STUDIES IN HISTORY, ECONOMICS AND PUBLIC LAW.

EDITED BY
THE UNIVERSITY FACULTY OF POLITICAL SCIENCE
OF COLUMBIA COLLEGE.

Volume I.] [Number 4.

THE

FINANCIAL HISTORY OF MASSACHUSETTS,

From the Organization of the Massachusetts Bay Company
to the American Revolution.

BY

CHARLES H. J. DOUGLAS, PH.D.,
Seligman Fellow in Political Science, Columbia College.

THE LAWBOOK EXCHANGE, LTD.
Clark, New Jersey
2005

ISBN 1-58477-572-6

Printed in the United States of America on acid-free paper

THE LAWBOOK EXCHANGE, LTD.
33 Terminal Avenue
Clark, New Jersey 07066-1321

Please see our website for a selection of our other publications and fine facsimile reprints of classic works of legal history:
www.lawbookexchange.com

Library of Congress Cataloging-in-Publication Data

Douglas, Charles Henry James, 1856-1931.
The financial history of Massachusetts : from the organization of the Massachusetts Bay Company to the American Revolution / Charles H.J. Douglas.
p. cm. — (Studies in history, economics and public law, v. 1, no. 4)
Originally published: New York : [Columbia University], 1892.
Originally presented as the author's thesis (doctoral)--Columbia University, 1892.
Includes bibliographical references.
ISBN 1-58477-572-6 (cloth : alk. paper)
1. Finance, Public--Massachusetts--History. I. Title. II. Series: Columbia studies in the social sciences, 4.
HJ495.D68 2005
336.744--dc22 2004042331

STUDIES IN HISTORY, ECONOMICS AND PUBLIC LAW.

EDITED BY
THE UNIVERSITY FACULTY OF POLITICAL SCIENCE
OF COLUMBIA COLLEGE.

Volume I.] [Number 4.

THE
FINANCIAL HISTORY OF MASSACHUSETTS,

From the Organization of the Massachusetts Bay Company to the American Revolution.

BY

CHARLES H. J. DOUGLAS, PH.D.,
Seligman Fellow in Political Science, Columbia College.

NEW YORK.
1892.

PREFACE.

To whatever degree the financial history of Massachusetts during the period of its dependency upon the British crown may be lacking in interest, as compared with the financial history of the commonwealth during the period of its membership in the American Union, I found that a patient and thorough investigation and a discriminating exposition of the financial phenomena of the earlier period were necessary antecedents to an intelligent investigation and interpretation of the far more complex financial phenomena of the later one. Viewed as chapters preliminary to the main discussion of the theme, I hope that the following pages will prove neither uninteresting nor uninstructive to those who would become acquainted with the facts in the financial history of one of the most conservative, at the same time that she is one of the most progressive, of American commonwealths. It is my purpose in a future essay to treat of the financial history of New England from the earliest settlement to the present time.

I offer no apology for any departure I may have made from the conventional treatment of financial themes, in the relatively large proportion of space which I have devoted to the exposition of administrative features, and the correspondingly small space to numerical statements, in the treatment of those periods in the history of Massachusetts when not only her financial legislation was taking permanent shape, but her financial records are all but worthless for purposes of accurate and valuable generalization, on account of their fragmentary and unsystematic character.

If the literary style which I have adopted appears at times

to be more involved than is ordinarily desirable, this is so because I could avoid it, even after limiting myself to a single period and to certain features fairly representative of the whole financial system of the commonwealth, only by resorting to one of two expedients,—either to emasculate my thought by omitting the expression of those frequently numerous and complex relationships upon which many of my central propositions depend, or to spin out the essay to an undue length in order to make the style perfectly simple. Considering the character of the readers for whom my work is intended, it did not seem to me that either of these alternatives was demanded.

C. H. J. D.

SCHOOL OF POLITICAL SCIENCE,
COLUMBIA COLLEGE,
February, 1892.

TABLE OF CONTENTS.

THE

FINANCIAL HISTORY OF MASSACHUSETTS

FROM THE ORGANIZATION OF THE MASSACHUSETTS BAY COMPANY TO THE AMERICAN REVOLUTION.

INTRODUCTION.

§ 1. *Massachusetts in history.*

The figure of Massachusetts is no unfamiliar one upon the stage of history. She has in fact occupied a prominent position there on many important occasions; and if her audience have not always been able to express an unqualified approval of her choice of parts, they have at least not failed to be impressed with the wide range of her histrionic capabilities, or with the intensity with which she impersonates the character of the hour. It is generally conceded that in the varied and trying rôles of persecutor of the heretic and champion of the slave, of punisher of witchcraft at home and defier of oppression abroad, Massachusetts has had few equals and no superiors. But there is another rôle in which she made her début at an early day, for the adequate sustaining of which, though it is far less spectacular than any of those above mentioned, unremitting rehearsal and many public performances during a period of over two hundred and fifty years have scarcely sufficed to prepare this venerable histrionic dame. The performance of Massachusetts as public financier demands our attention.

§ 2. *Periods of Financial History.*

The American revolution marks a natural division of the history of Massachusetts into two periods, each with financial characteristics distinct from those of the other:—the period of her dependency upon the British crown, and the period of her membership in the American union. The first of these periods again divides itself into two others, corresponding to the respective lives of the colonial and provincial charters; while the second, though shaken by no such violent political tempests as served to break up the previous history of the commonwealth into epochs, is marked near its middle by the beginning of that great and varied material development which, during the last half century, has completely changed the character of the science of finance in all civilized countries. We thus have four well-defined periods of financial history. The present monograph is devoted to the first two of these periods, comprising the larger one of the dependency of the commonwealth upon the British crown.

BOOK I.

THE COLONY OF MASSACHUSETTS BAY.

§ 3. *Beginnings of Massachusetts.*

Whether the commowealth of Massachusetts is to be regarded as having had its real origin at the landing of the Pilgrims at Cape Cod in 1620, or at the moment when the Company of the Massachusetts Bay purchased of the Council at Plymouth the title to the vast and vaguely defined territory within the bounds of which the present state of Massachusetts lies, or on the granting of a charter by Charles II. to the Governor and Company of the Massachusetts Bay in 1628, or on the arrival of Winthrop out of England with the charter itself in 1630, is a question in constitutional law rather than in finance.[1] If any of the above views other than the last be taken, we have, prior to the beginning of Winthrop's adminministration, a period properly embraced within the history of the commonwealth, presenting a body of fiscal material and suggesting lines of financial investigation which offer to the student of finance a high degree of interest. The present dis-

[1]On November 3rd, 1620, King James signed a patent by which the adventurers to the northern colony of Virginia between forty and forty-eight degrees north latitude, were incorporated as the Council Established at Plymouth in the County of Devon, for the Planting, Ruling, Ordering and Governing of New England in America. This is the great civil basis of the future patents and plantations of the country. See the text of the patent in Hazard's Collection of State Papers, I., 103. On March 19th, 1627, the Council at Plymouth sold to some knights and gentlemen about Dorchester that part of their patent which lay between the Charles and Merimack rivers. It was to these persons, or to their successors, that King Charles, in 1628, granted a charter incorporating them into a body politic under the style of the Governor and Company of the Massachusetts Bay in New England.

cussion begins with some account of the Massachusetts company.

§ 4. *The Massachusetts Company.*

Concerning the original form of organization of the Massachusetts Bay Company, little information is known to exist. It was probably similar to that of the company who about that time settled at New Plymouth, and who, as we know from the testimony of Capt. John Smith, although they had a capital stock of at least £7000, were not a corporation, but knit together by voluntary combination. The Plymouth Company had a president and a treasurer who were chosen annually by the majority and who ordered the affairs of the courts and meetings and undertook all ordinary business, though in more weighty affairs the assent of the whole company was required. No records of the colony that was sent over by the Massachusetts Company, belonging to Endicott's administration, have been preserved; but Governor Bradford, of New Plymouth, in a letter written June 9th, 1628, mentions a sort of voluntary tax by which various individuals and places in the Bay assessed themselves in certain sums bearing no common proportion to their respective means, and amounting to £12 7s.[1]

We have record also of an appeal by the officers of the Massachusetts Company, as early as June 17th, 1629,[2] while the charter and government were still in England, to the members as individuals to advance to the company such sums as they might be able to spare, toward extinguishing a debt of the company, receiving therefor receipts under the company seal. In this and subsequent similar acts we have the first steps in that development of enforced contribution, or taxation, out of voluntary contribution, which the financial history

1 Plymouth, £2 10s; Naumkeak, £1 10s; Pascataquack, £2 10s; Mr. Jeffrey and Mr. Burslem, £2; Nastascot, £1 10s; Mr. Thomson, 15s; Mr. Blackston, 12s; Edward Hilton, £1. Total, £12 7s.

2 Massachusetts Records, I., 47.

of every organized society presents. It appears from a letter of the company in London to Endicott, May 28th, 1629, that they required of all emigrants hither, who received lands but made no payment to the common stock, a sort of service tax, which, exacting of each colonist and his heirs who held landed estates in this manner a specified number of days' labor each year, bore some resemblance to tenure of socage in England. The income to the government from this source was in reality less a tax than it was the price of a portion of the public domain, alienated on terms which the purchaser could have declined, had he so elected. It is probable that the arrangement was soon abandoned; the above reference to it being the only one thus far discovered.

§ 5. *The Genesis of the Taxing Power.*

The probability arising from the foregoing facts that the Massachusetts Company lacked altogether the power generally vested in stock companies of levying assessments upon their stockholders is rendered more certain by the fact that not only on the occasion above mentioned, when the company was £1500 behind in its accounts, but also in the following November, when it was more than £3000 in debt, no record has been found of any proposition to levy an assessment upon the members, although on both of these occasions various extraordinary measures were proposed for raising funds.[1] If the company itself had no power of assessment, that is of taxation, it is clear that it could grant no such power to a colony organized among its members and sent out under its direction.

[1] An exhaustive account of the fortunes of the original shareholders of the Massachusetts Company is yet to be written, Mr. Samuel F. Haven's short introduction to the reprint of the records of the company for the first thirteen years, contained in Vol. III. of the Transactions of the American Antiquarian Society, being chiefly devoted to an account of the shareholders themselves. Much material for this interesting chapter of the financial history of Massachusetts exists, though in a chirography likely to try severely the patience of the investigator, in Vol. 100 of Felt's collection of Massachusetts Archives.

The vote of the court of assistants of the Massachusetts colony, at their third meeting in America,[1] levying a tax upon all the freemen of the colony, was thus clearly an act of usurpation, which became legitimate only by the acquiescence of every freeman so rated. The power to tax having once become in the government of Massachusetts a *fait accompli*—which the charter of Charles II. ignored and that of William and Mary confirmed—we are henceforth concerned only with the history of taxation as an integral part of the fiscal policy of that government.

§ 6. *The Development of Taxation.*

It is to the triumph of the proselyting over the mercantile spirit among the members of the company in London that we are to attribute the selection, October 20th, 1629, for the important duty of transferring the charter and government of the company itself to New England, of John Winthrop, a man who, however well educated he may have been in the learning of his day, however amiable in domestic and social relations, in a word was too intently devoted to recording prodigies of three-headed calves[2] to give adequate attention to the management of his own property, to say nothing of developing an original financial policy for the colony over which he presided with suave and conscientious tyranny.[3] The tendency of colonists in all times merely to reproduce upon new soil the institutions of the mother country was allowed full play in Massachusetts by the absence on the part of the early governors of any positive interest in, if not by the presence in them of actual con-

[1] On September 28th, 1630.

[2] See Winthrop's History of New England II., 311.

[3] Hutchinson, speaking of Winthrop's being called sharply to account for his financial transactions while governor, says that he "might have torn his book of accounts, as Scipio Africanus did, and given the ungrateful people this answer: A colony now in a flourishing state has been led out and settled under my direction. My own substance is consumed. Spend no more time in harangues, but give thanks to God."—Hutchinson, History of Massachusetts, I., 140.

tempt for, all financial concerns. Accordingly we find introduced, as a matter of course, as one exigency after another called for successive increases in the public revenue, the general property tax, imposts, excises, the capitation tax, the income tax and taxes on certain specified classes of property—all of them forms of taxation with which the colonists had already become familiar in England. Indeed, so conservative have the people been that these remained the only forms resorted to, not only during the colonial and provincial periods, but long after Massachusetts became a state independent of the British crown.

§ 7. *The Property Tax.*

Unlike the imposts and excises that constituted almost the sole sources of revenue for their commercial neighbors in New Netherland,[1] the backbone of the loose-jointed fiscal organization which, prior to the middle of the seventeenth century, had become sufficiently developed among the farmers of Massachusetts Bay to admit of its identification, was a general property tax, levied at first as the occasion of the hour demanded, and afterward with greater regularity,[2] upon the estates of the freemen of the colony. The machinery for assessing and collecting this tax was as simple as the theory underlying the assessment was just; and neither theory nor machinery underwent much, if any, alteration during the colonial period. Indeed, as we shall see in subsequent sections, it was essentially the colonial system of taxation that extended quite through the provincial period, and even well into the present century.

§ 8. *Apportionment, Repartition and Assessment.*

The first step in the history of one of these early colonial property taxes was the apportionment among the various

[1] Schwab, History of the New York Property Tax, 19.

[2] The act of November 24th, 1646, first provided for yearly taxes.

towns of the colony of the sum granted by the general court to be raised. At first the apportionment was made by the general court itself in proportions agreed upon among the deputies, who, as long as the number of towns in the colony remained small, had a better knowledge than any one else of the value of the property in each. But the growth of the colony in wealth and population soon rendering this plan unsatisfactory, an act of May 16th, 1636, named thirteen freemen of the colony as a committee "with power to require the last rates of each town in the plantation, and find out thereby and by all other means they can, according to the best of their discretion, the true value of every town and so to make an equal rate"—the committee to meet in Boston on a day appointed in the act, and there to determine the apportionment. As evidenced by numerous references, this plan was continued as late at least as 1640, on May 13th of which year a rate of £1200 was granted and the usual apportionment committee appointed.

There are reasons for believing that for the first sixteen years of the existence of the colony the repartition among the taxpayers of the quotas determined for the towns by the general court and the apportionment committees was made by the selectmen of the respective towns. The principle upon which assessments were to be made was laid down by the general court as early as May 14th, 1634: "In all rates and public charges the towns [through their assessors] shall have respect to levy every man according to his estate, and with consideration all other his abilities whatsoever, and not according to the number of his persons."[1] The language of the acts of this and of later periods is often ambiguous, and there is no reason for supposing that the ideas of their framers, upon fiscal matters, were either very definite or very systematic. An order of the general court under date of May 3d, 1636, "explains" an order of May, 1634, according to which all men were "to be

[1] Massachusetts Records, I., 168.

rated in all rates according to their whole ability wheresoever it lyes," by enacting that thenceforth "all men that live in this jurisdiction be rated only in the place where they live to all public rates, and those that live not in this jurisdiction are to have their goods, stocks and lands rated where they are in being."[1] June 6th, 1639, an act was passed declaring that estates in England should be taxed for what they were worth;[2] but this was repealed two years later.[3]

§ 9. *Taxpayers; Exemptions.*

The restriction of taxation to freemen of the colony resulted, as long as all the adult male inhabitants of the colony were freemen, in manhood taxation. When the number of men who were debarred from becoming freemen because they were not church members, and who thus escaped taxation altogether, had become so large that the manhood basis began to be seriously impaired, the colonial government took a further step in the extension of their prerogative and in the development of taxation from voluntary contribution, by enacting that all male inhabitants above the age of sixteen years, whether church members or not, "servant or other," must contribute to the common charges; and that if they did not do so voluntarily, they must be assessed and compelled to. In 1665[4] the court declared that so many strangers came into the colony with cargoes, which they disposed of in time to depart before the next tax, that thereafter the cargoes should be taxed when they came in; that if the owners refused to disclose the value of them, the goods should be "doomed," and the collectors should be given power to distrain them.

From the beginning, certain exemptions to the general rule of taxation were made. Sometimes the exemption would be

[1] Massachusetts Records, I., 168.

[2] *Ibid.* 262.

[3] *Ibid.* 330.

[4] May 3rd.

made on account of poverty resulting from old age, sickness, lameness, blindness, or such other infirmity as appeared to the selectmen to disable the man from contributing. Sometimes it was regarded as a partial or complete compensation for public services, as in the case of troopers,[1] of magistrates to the extent of £500[2] and of professors in Harvard College to the extent of £100 personal property[3]. At other times exemptions were accorded for the encouragement of enterprises likely to prove of public benefit, such as the fisheries,[4] from time to time, and the iron works set up in Braintree;[5] or as pure gratuities, as when the exemption on account of age, at first confined to individual cases, was extended to all inhabitants over sixty years old, on the supposition of the general inability of such persons to contribute. It is impossible from any data known to exist to ascertain the exact proportion of all these exemptions to the whole population of the colony; but probably it was small. A more serious factor in disturbing the universality of taxation was the custom which prevailed from a very early time, of partially or wholly exempting, by special enactments, for several years at a time, towns newly settled or lately ravaged by the Indians.[6] A remonstrance of the town of Boston to the general court in September, 1653,

[1] The practice of exempting troopers existed before 1648. July 9th, 1675, troopers not exempt from rates for Indian war. October 13th, troopers' exemption limited to one rate annually. Massachusetts Records, V., 49, 94-5.

[2] May 14th, 1645, Massachusetts Records, II., 101; November 4th, 1646.

[3] Massachusetts Records, IV., 537. They were more fully exempted by the act of June 19th, 20th, 1754-'5, c. 11.

[4] Massachusetts Records, I., 257.

[5] March 7th, 1643-'4, Massachusetts Records, II., 62.

[6] May 14th, 1656, Groton freed for three years from the date of the grant. Massachusetts Records, IV., Pt. I., 262.—June, 1661, Springfield and Northampton rate free one year, to build prison to cost not less than £60. Massachusetts Records, IV., Pt. II., 21.—June 3d, 1674, Southfield exempt for four years. Massachusetts Records, V., 13.—October 12th, 1676, abatements to Medfield, Weymouth, Hingham, Sudbury, Concord, Chelmsford, Andover, Springfield, Northampton and Hadley; but one to Hampshire refused. Massachusetts Records, V., 122 *et seq.*

against the exemption of magistrates, passed unheeded. On November 2d, 1680, the deputies passed an order that thereafter "no person of what quality soever" should be exempted from the country rates for either his person or his estate, except such persons as were disabled by sickness, lameness or other bodily infirmity, who should be exempted for their persons only, and elders regularly ordained over churches, who should be exempted for estates of their own, under their own management.[1] This vote, evidently aimed at the magistrates, was lost by the non-concurrence of that body. On the whole, there seems to have been no general or long-continued dissatisfaction on account of exemptions during the period under review.

§ 10. *Collection: Officers; Difficulties.*

The machinery for collecting taxes in Massachusetts was from the earliest times exceedingly simple. It may have been the fact that the constable was already "armed with very large powers, of arresting and impressing, of breaking open houses and the like,"[2] to the end that he might the more successfully perform his general duty of keeping the king's peace in his district, which first suggested him to our ancestors in England as the most natural officer to whom to commit the collection of taxes—a duty in the performance of which it would be necessary, in certain cases, to have recourse to the legal process of distress, or even to imprisonment. Although the first tax act of the court of assistants of the Massachusetts Bay Company in America[3] fails to name the officer who should collect the tax, it is evident from the facts that it was to "be collected and levied by distress," and that for many years afterward no officer except the constable is mentioned in connection with collections, that the duties of that ancient

[1] Felt's Massachusetts Archives, Vol. 100, p. 262.

[2] Blackstone, Commentaries, I., 356.

[3] September 28th, 1630.

officer transplanted to New England, as far as they concerned financial matters, had not been abridged by the colonists, and that from the very beginning he held in the financial system of Massachusetts the position which he continues to hold to-day. The difficulty of collecting the taxes at this early period is attested not only by the impowering of the officer to distrain for them,[1] but by the beginning, as early as 1636, of the practice of dividing a tax granted into two or more payments, several months apart,[2] and by the specific mention of arrears in acts of 1643 and various subsequent years and in various documents throughout the colonial period.[3] It was largely this difficulty that led to the introduction of excises and imposts in 1644,[4] and to various adjustments of the tariff at subsequent times, with a view to lessening the property tax.[5]

§ 11. *The United Colonies.*

We are not surprised to find the principle of taxation according to ability to pay, upon which the Massachusetts system was thus early grounded and which was recognized in all the New England colonies, embodied in the articles of confedera-

[1] Massachusetts Records, I., 239.

[2] Sometimes, as in the case above cited, September 7th, 1636, the second payment would be postponed to a time to be determined by the court in the future; in which case it usually happened that the time was never fixed and the payment never made.

[3] The report of the committee to audit the treasurer's accounts, 1669–'70, mentions great delinquency in the payment of taxes outside of Boston and Charlestown. Felt's Massachusetts Archives, Vol. 100, pp. 147–154.

[4] November 13th.

[5] "The Magts being sensible that the Inhabitants of this Iurisdiction do in many respects Labour under those difficultyes which make the taxes of the country (though small comparatively) to be a great burden, do judge meet that a comittee be named & appoynted by this Court to consider of some expedient for help therein, by addition to customes, or other ways in such wise as may not discourage the trade & marchandize of the Country, and for yt end doe name," etc. This vote was lost by the non-concurrence of the deputies. See Felt's Massachusetts Archives, Vol. 100, p. 176.

tion adopted in August, 1643, by the colonies of Massachusetts, Plymouth, Connecticut and New Haven. The article relating to the raising of troops and funds for the commissioners of the United Colonies reads as follows:

"It is by these confederats agreed that the charge of all just warrs, whether offensiue or defensiue, upon what part or member of this confederacon soeuer they fall, shall both in men and provisions and all other disbursements, be borne by all the parts of this confederacon in different proporcons according to their different abilitie. And that according to the different members, which from tyme to tyme shalbe formed in eich jurisdiccon, upon a true and just account, the service of men and all charges of warr be borne by the polls: eich jurisdiccon or plantacon being left to their own just course and custome of rating themselues and people according to their differant estates, with due respect to their quallities and exemptions among themselves, though the confederacon take no notice of any such priviledg: and that according to their different charge of eich jurisdiccon and plantacon, the whole advantage of the warr (if it please God to bless their endeavours) whether it be in lands, goods or persons, shalbe proportionably divided among the said confederats."[1]

§ 12. *Efforts toward Improvement.*

From all the foregoing it is sufficiently evident that the system of taxation in operation in Massachusetts Bay, never yet very effective, was every day becoming less adequate to the needs of a now rapidly growing colony. There was a feeling that it was the constables who were at fault; and on November 13th, 1645, the general court, in a spasm of administrative reform ordered them—"Every constable that now is or hereafter hath binn"— to clear up their accounts with the treasurer by the first of May yearly, on penalty of being fined £5 apiece; and they were given the power of impressing boats and carts to enable them to transport the commodities in which the taxes might be paid.[2] Under date of October 7th, 1646, the

[1] Hazard, II., 2, 3; quoted by Felt, Statistics, 230.

[2] Massachusetts Records, IV., Pt. I., 247.

general court, considering that it had incurred the necessary expense of sending an agent to England, and that the treasurer reported no money in the treasury, recorded its conviction that the constables, marshals, auditor or treasurer were to blame, and chose a committee of three to investigate the matter and prosecute the delinquents. We have seen no account of the report of this committee; but within less than a month, on November, 4th 1646, an act was passed which is here subjoined in full, because, simple as it is, it yet placed the whole tax system on a more scientific footing, and so marks the beginning of a new period in the financial history of the colony.

"For ye avoiding of all complaints by reason of unequal rates either of towns or psons, occasioned through ye want of one gen^{r}all way and rule of rateing through out ye country, and y^{t} levies hereafter may be more easy, equall, and certeine, it is hereby ordered, y^{t} in all publike rates (till this Co^{r}te take further order therein) all sortes of cattle shalbe valued as hereafter exprest * * * * houses, lands of all sorts, marchantable goods, mills, shipps, lesser vessels and boates, cranes, wharfes, togeth^{r} wth all oth^{r} visible estate, reall or psonal, y^{t} any pson is possessed of, or hath in his custody, eith^{r} at sea or on shore, to be valued in ye severall townes according to their worth, in ye said places where they are, pportionable to ye aforesaid prizes of cattle; and it is ye meaning of this order y^{t} because arable ground, medowe, and cattle are to be rated, y^{t} therefore they, together wth all corne growing in ye country, in ye husbandmans hand, shall not be lyable to any rate; and for avoyding all partiality in rating lands and oth^{r} estate not pticularly prized in this ord^{r}, it is ordered y^{t} y^{r} shalbe by ev^{ry} towne one of their inhabitants chosen by ye freemen of ye said towne, who, wth ye select townes men shall take the iust numb^{r} of their males, and also shall make a true valuation of all things rateable by this order, wch inhabitants aforsaid, for their severall townes respectively, shall meet in their shire townes upon ye 2th 4th day of ye first month next ensuing, to examine ye truth and equity of each towns pceeding herein, who shall correct and determine as to the maior pt of them seems right and iust to be done, according to ye true intent of this order; wch assesm^{ts} of ye severall townes they shall und^{r} their hands fortwith deliv^{r} to ye Treasurer, who shall also forthwth send forth his warrants for leviing ye same wthin one month, whereby he may have to answere ye engagem^{ts} of ye country; and assesm^{ts} for estates shall hereafter be made ye first 4th day of ye 6th m^{o,} from time to time; but all levies for ye psons shalbe made and paid into ye treasury in ye first m^{o,} fro^{m} year to yeare, as is pvided in ye order aforesaid."[1]

§ 13. *Further Reforms.*

So well does the reform thus inaugurated appear to have worked that an act of October 27th, 1647, instructed the colonial treasurer to send out notice every fifth month without further instruction, to the constable and selectmen of every town, requiring the constable to call together the inhabitants, who should elect one of their freemen to be commissioner, who together with the selectmen should make out a tax-list, submit it to the examination of the freemen and, after correction, transmit it to the treasurer as provided by the act of the previous year. The act further provided that if any commissioner or selectman were found guilty of neglect or falsifying, he should be fined forty shillings for each offence. Another section became the corollary of the act of May 16th, 1636, declaring that, inasmuch as so many owners of real estate living in the towns departed from them every year just in time to escape being taxed, thereafter all real property should be taxed where it lay. Partly as a wise precaution against collusion between the assessors and the treasurer, and partly to give a newly-created officer, the auditor-general, something to do, an act of May 10th, 1648, provided that the commissioners of the towns should transmit, within one month after their meetings in these towns, true transcripts of their tax-lists to the auditor-general, who should deliver them to the treasurer, to be collected as before. But now that an effort to render the tax system more effective was really beginning to be

[1] Massachusetts Records, II., 174–'5.

made, it was not long before enough weak points in that system were discovered. Already the fundamental defect of a general property tax—a defect that becomes more fatal as a community makes industrial progress—was beginning to be painfully evident; and we have the commencement of that series of skirmishes so familiar to the student of taxation, between the tax-layers on the one hand and the tax-payers on the other, in which the former find themselves impelled to more and more drastic measures for discovering and dragging out before the assessors the ever-multiplying forms of intangible personal property, and the latter are rather diverted than embarrassed by the necessity of devising means for evading every new turn of their pursuers. The first move of the game in Massachusetts was made by the legislature, May 7th, 1651:

"To the end that all public charges may be equally borne, and that some may not to be eased and other burdened, and being found by experience that visible estates in lands, corn, cattle, are, according to rule, wholly and fairly taxed, but the estates of merchants, in the hands of neighbors and strangers, or their factors, are not so obvious to view, but, upon search, title of these estates do appear, being of great value, so that the law doth not reach them by that rule of taxing visible estates, it is therefore ordered and enacted by this court and the authority thereof that all merchants, shopkeepers and factors shall be assessed by the rule of common estimation, according to the will and doom of the assessors in such cases appointed, having regard to their stock and estate, be it presented to view or not, in whose hands soever it be, that such great estates as come yearly into the country may bear their proportion in public charges; yet if any find themselves overvalued, if they can make it appear to the assessors, they are to be eased by them; if not, by the next court."

§ 14. *Attempts at Equalization.*

An act of May 6th, 1657, declares that "Whereas it is evident that there is much injustice and inequality in the assessment of public rates in each town within this jurisdiction, whereby some are eased, others burdened, and the commonwealth prejudiced, for the prevention thereof it is ordered that houses and lands of all sorts shall be rated at an equal and indifferent value according to their worth in the towns where they lie." This seems to show that the comparative unavailability of real estate as a basis for general, as opposed to local, taxation was already beginning to be felt with the expansion of the province. On April 29th, 1668, a commission consisting of six members was appointed to visit each county, meeting the commissioners from all the towns therein, at a particular place in the county, to examine and equalize the lists. On May 15th, the commission reported that they had visited all the counties, and, though much embarrassed by the imperfection of the lists, had performed their duties by raising or lowering the taxes in various towns, according to their judgment, in the spirit and letter of the law.[1] On October 21st, 1669, "the commissioners of the several shire towns," having met, according to the order of the court and having perfected the assessments of the several towns, and transcribed them to the colony treasurer, now petition the court for their pay.[2] Finally, on October 11th, 1682, the court declared that so many farms are laid out outside of the towns and so pay no rates though the land is rising in value, the owners of such farms must thereafter pay two shillings per one hundred acres, the selectmen of each town to take account of all such farms lying near their towns.[3]

§ 15. *Rate and "Rates."*

The materials for ascertaining the rate of taxation under the first charter, while they are not complete for the first few years, become much fuller after 1650. In the absence of positive contemporary evidence it may be presumed that the propor-

[1] Original report in Felt's Massachusetts Archives, Vol. 100, p. 127.

[2] Massachusetts Records, IV., Pt. 2., 444.

[3] Massachusetts Records, V., 376.

tion of one penny to every twenty shillings of the value of estates, which had become the usual rate before 1646, and which by the act of November 4th in that year was established by the general court as the legal rate upon "lands and goods," was fixed upon as the proportion which, in the light of experience, ought to yield a sum nearly or quite sufficient to meet the public expenses, when reckoned upon the property of the colony and taken together with the proceeds of the poll tax. Certainly the inhabitants of the colony were good enough mathematicians to know that in a computation in which the base and the rate per cent. are both fixed quantities the product is also a fixed quantity; but if they hoped, by fixing upon an unvarying rate to be applied annually to the property in the colony, to limit the expenditure by the government to the sum thus obtained, it was not long before the futility of their attempt was manifest. The ingenuity of the colonial legislators was, however, sufficient for the emergency that arose when it became evident that the whole amount of property in the colony, as returned by the commissioners, was not increasing at as rapid a rate as the public expenses were. From the passage of the act of November 13th, 1655, which ordered one and one-quarter rates to be laid, the one penny per every twenty shillings ceased to be *the* rate and became a "rate." It was the old scheme of reduplication that had long before been practiced in England in multiplying the tenths and fifteenths. In Massachusetts not only was the rate of the "rate" thus increased, but the early practice of making more than one levy per year was revived when occasion demanded. On the other hand, in 1670 only "half a rate" was levied; and in 1672 it was ordered[1] that no rate at all be levied, as the income from wines, peltry, etc., was sufficient to meet the public expenses. From this time on till the loss of the charter the rates were added to or multiplied year by year, the number rising in some years as high as sixteen, noticeably in 1676

[1] Act of October 8th, 1672.

to meet the expenses of King Philip's war. The average for the whole time was not far from four. Yet the pleasing theory was still maintained that the regular rate was but one penny per pound, and the assessors found themselves relieved by the legislature of one of their most disagreeable duties.

§ 16. *The Poll Tax.*

By far the most interesting feature of Massachusetts finances under the first charter is the poll tax. What has already been said of the simplicity of the machinery for assessing and collecting the property tax is equally true of the poll tax; in fact, the machinery for both the taxes was identical, both being apportioned and assessed by the same body, though at first at different times of the year, and collected together in a single sum. The poll tax entered, together with the property and faculties taxes, as a component element into the sums which the deputies apportioned among the towns. The taxpayers and exemptions were the same as in the case of the property tax. The rate, too, in the case of polls, was regarded as being the same as that in the case of property, viz., one penny per pound. But instead of ascertaining by inquiry the money value of each unit to be assessed, as was done in the case of the property tax, an arbitrary sum was taken as the common value of each adult male poll in the colony—a theory sufficiently democratic, one would suppose, to satisfy the demands of the most uncompromising social leveler. By the important act of November 4th, 1646, already referred to, and the first rule upon this point which we have seen, the amount of the poll tax was placed at twenty pence for each taxpayer—the base upon which it was reckoned being, of course, twenty pounds. There is reason for believing that the same figure had then been in use from the beginning of the poll tax in Massachusetts. The next year, October 27th, 1647, the rate of the poll tax was raised to two shillings six pence; but August 30th, 1653, a return was made to the old rate, and

November 7th, 1690, the tax was reduced to twelve pence for each "rate."

§ 17. *The Reduplication of Poll Taxes.*

It is not, however, in these particulars that the chief interest of the Massachusetts colonial poll tax lies to students of finance. That interest attaches to the amounts, astonishing enough, whether considered absolutely or in comparison with the corresponding amounts yielded by the property tax, which were exacted from each male inhabitant of the colony under the system of reduplication of rates already described. It was certainly an unfortunate day for all but the wealthiest colonists of Massachusetts when the expedient of reduplicating rates was applied to them; for it must be understood—and here lies the point of the whole matter—that the doubling, or trebling, or quadrupling of a "rate" meant the doubling, or trebling, or quadrupling, not only of the property tax, but of the poll tax as well; and, the poll tax being the same for rich and poor alike, the inequality of any reduplication increased in geometrical ratio, in favor of or against the taxpayer, according as he possessed more or less than the average amount of property for each taxpayer. An attempt of the writer to collect sufficient data from which to construct a continuous diagram, showing the actual amount of the poll tax in Massachusetts for each year, from the beginning to 1680, has thus far proved unsuccessful. Such a table would convey better than can any verbal description an idea of the state of things that drew from the long-suffering townsmen of Boston in 1653 a petition, one of the most valuable of our early financial documents, in which they truly say: "In respect of polle money we apprehend its parallel is not in any country where the sword is not drawn in offensive or defensive war."[1] But although the petitioners make in their memorial four propositions looking toward the more equable distribution of taxes, they offer no

[1] Original petition in Massachusetts Archives, Vol. 100, p. 44.

suggestion touching a reform of the poll tax. Even the expedient, only partially effective in practice and no more just in principle, of reducing the rate of the poll tax for each "rate," as was done in 1689, appears not to have occurred to any one of these petitioners; and the practice of reduplicating poll taxes, the most grossly inequitable of any feature of colonial taxation in Massachusetts, was continued till with the better organization of the finances under the second charter it was finally discarded.

§ 18. *The Faculties Tax.*

Notwithstanding the general impression that property and poll taxes were the only forms of direct taxation practiced in colonial Massachusetts, what is to all intents and purposes an income tax, partial, indeed, in its operation—as what income taxes have not been?—but yet a veritable income tax, is found as early as 1646. The important tax law of November 4th of that year, so often referred to in the preceding pages, beside providing for a property and a poll tax, declares that "every laborer, artificer, etc., that takes over 18d. per day in summer time, or works by greate that averages over 18d. per day, shall pay 3s. 4d. over and above the 20d. [poll tax] beforesaid;" and that others, not particularly mentioned, such as smiths and the like, shall be "rated proportionable to the produce of the estates of other men," provided the usual exemptions for inability to contribute are made. Here we have the principle of the income tax applied to two classes of incomes from "faculties," as the expression then was. In an act of the next year, October 27th, 1647, the 3s–4d. class was omitted, and all those enumerated were taxed on the capitalized value of their wages. This income tax, as long as it lasted—the phrase referring to "faculties" is retained in the Massachusetts tax acts to this day—was assessed, levied and collected by the same officials and at the same time as the property and the poll taxes were. On account of this commingling there is no way of ascertaining what amounts the faculties tax itself yielded to the treasury. It appears to have been regarded by all concerned as merely an adjunct of the property tax.

§ 19. *Indirect Taxes.*

It is worth noting that the order of the succession of the general forms of taxation in Massachusetts is the reverse of that in New York. There the general property tax was tardily introduced as a means of easing the burden of indirect taxation, especially that of the excise;[1] here indirect taxes—excises and imposts—were introduced as a means of easing the burden of direct taxation. But direct taxation remained throughout the colonial and provincial periods the principal source of public revenue. In Massachusetts the legislation of the period relating to excises and imposts is so crudely empirical that it defies all attempts at such an analysis as would serve for a basis upon which to formulate the details of the system—if anything so lacking in articulation may be called a system—that grew up under it. There was throughout the colonial period no separate administrative organization for either imposts or excises, the colonial treasurer generally being designated, either alone or in association with one or two other inhabitants, to administer the separate laws as they were passed;[2] while the auditor-general, during the brief existence of that office, was sometimes called upon to assist in the collection of the duties.[3] Further than this generalization, the best that can be done is to give brief synopses of the most important excise and impost laws in chronological order.

1 Schwab, History of the New York Property Tax, p. 22 *et seq.*

2 For example: May 19th, 1680, the General Court ordered that James Russell, treasurer, have the whole collection of the rates on wines, liquors, etc., this year, as Paul Dudley had last year, and that John Dudley and John Richards assist him in making contracts, etc.—Felt's Massachusetts Archives, Vol. 100, p. 142.

3 Thus he was empowered, May 6th, 1646, to break open cellars and seize smuggled liquors.

§ 20. *The Progress of Legislation.*

On June 2d, 1641, a charge is laid on the beaver trade. On November 13th, 1644, it is ordered that every vintner and other person having a license to draw wine be taxed twenty shillings per butt or sack, and be required to appear before the general court four times per year to swear as to the quantity sold by him and to pay for the same; also, that all wines wholesaled into the country pay the same rate.[1] On October 1st, 1645, English ships and such others as "free us" are exempted from tonnage.[2] On November 4th, 1646, all retailers of wine must pay such a license fee as the court judge proper.[3] On October 27th, 1647, companies for trading with the Indians must pay two pence for every skin purchased.[4] On May 10th, 1648, to increase the revenue, stricter regulations as to the wine customs are promulgated.[5] On May 2d, 1649, a schedule of customs on imports and exports between Boston and Plymouth, New Haven and Connecticut is adopted.[6] On May 30th, 1650, customs to confederate colonies are suspended till the commissioners act.[7] On October 26th, 1652, the old contract on wine impost expiring, all bidders for a new one are required to meet the deputies and agree upon terms.[8] On May 19th, 1658, stricter regulations as to imposts are provided; farmers of wine imposts are eased and discharged.[9] On April 29th, 1668, the treasurer is authorized to farm imposts, beaver trade, excise (wine, malt liquors, etc.) and ammunition trade.[10]

1 Massachusetts Records, II., 82.

2 *Ibid.*, II., 130.

3 *Ibid.*, II., 173.

4 *Ibid.*, II., 173.

5 *Ibid.*, II., 246–'7.

6 *Ibid.*, II., 269.

7 *Ibid.*, IV., Pt. I., 11.

8 *Ibid.*, IV., Pt. I., 111.

9 *Ibid.*, IV., Pt. I., 327.

10 *Ibid.*, IV., Pt. I., 327.

§ 21. *The Systemization of Imposts.*

By far the most important financial legislation of the colony after the systemization of the property tax was that of June 4th, 1669, under the title "Impost." The reason for this act, as assigned in the preamble, was the receipt by the court "of sundry Complaints of much Inequality in the present way of raising Moneys to defray Public Charges." All goods "excepting Fish, Sheeps-wool, Cotton-wool, Salt, and such other things as by former Laws are exempted, or otherwise provided for," were now to pay "a just proportion with Estates Rateable in the Country," viz., one penny for every twenty shillings' value—the value to be ascertained by adding twenty per cent. to the value at the place whence imported. The "Master, Purser, Boatswain, or Skipper of each Ship," upon its entering port, and "before breaking Bulk, or Landing any of the said Goods," must certify their value "unto the Country[1] Treasurer or Collector by him impowred." The collector should thereupon enter in a book kept for that purpose "all such Goods, with their several Marks, Casks, Packs, Fardels, Trusses, Chests, Trunks, Cases, and all other things however called or distinguished," and the name of the consignee. Before landing any goods, the owner or importer should "signifie the true and just value thereof, by showing the true and perfect Invoice thereof," to the collector, who should enter the gross sum in his book, and "forthwith demand and receive" the proper rates. "In case of denial or delay of payment, the collector" should distrain the goods. If the invoice were "falsified, concealed, or not produced," "the Treasurer or Collector, with the Select Men of each Town therein concerned," should rate the goods "by Will and Doom, according to their best discretion," but at a rate "not less than four pounds per Tun."

[1] Not to the *town* treasurer, as Dr. John Dean Goss says in The History of Tariff Administration in the United States, 15, in which he gives a good summary of the above-mentioned legislation, attributing it, however, to the following May.

"For all other sorts of Goods, Hides, Skins, Beaver, Peltry, Butter, Cheese, or other Merchandize," brought in by land, the rate should be one penny per pound, with similar administrative provisions. In difficult or doubtful cases, the officer should "repair to the Governour and Council," who should give directions for the removal of the obstructions.

§ 22. *Treasurers' Records.*

The absolutely chaotic condition of such scraps of accounts as the colonial treasurers have left on record renders fruitless the most patient and laborious attempt to work out from them any systematic statement of the colonial finances. Surely, the disembodied spirit of John Winthrop hovered over the treasurers' books for half a century after that venerable worthy ceased to preside in the colonial councils in his own proper person. After more than fifteen years, during which we have no evidence that any accounts at all were kept by the colonial treasurers, the general court made a move in the direction of securing better financial records. "Whereas," run the minutes under date of October 18th, 1645, "this court hath found by much experience what damage the country sustains for want of keeping exact accounts of all moneys that is due to the country, either by gifts, fines, rates, legacies and otherwise, as also of moneys issuing from the country upon several occasions, they have thought fit this 15th of the 8th month, 1645, to elect and make choice of Leift. Nathaniel Duncan to be auditor-general for this country, and have conferred upon him £30 per annum during the pleasure of the court, and he to give account as often as called by the court."

§ 23. *Duties of the Auditor-General.*

The specifications of the auditor-general's duty that follow under thirteen heads mapped out a wide field of activity for an official from whom great things in the way of financial reform were evidently expected. He was (1) to allow no bill which did not rightly belong to the colony to pay, or which more properly belonged to other colonies, towns or persons; and being in doubt he was to suspend payment till he could apply to the court; (2) to examine all notes, bills and accounts against the country and agree with those who presented them if the rate seemed too high or no agreement had previously been made; also to pass no bills to the treasurer unless accompanied by vouchers and signatures of such persons as had received or taken up the things for which the country was charged, as ferryages, diet, etc., the treasurer on his part to pay no bill not signed by the auditor-general, who was to be the judge between the creditor and the country, to see that no wrong was done to either; (3) to keep accounts of all his transactions; to summon all creditors of the country to render their accounts and all debtors to pay what they owed, on the pain of prosecution if they failed to do so; (4) to notify the country that all that brought suits in the general court must settle according to the order of the court; (5) to take note of the rates and how they were apportioned among the towns, and make the treasurer debtor for the same; in case of discrepancy between his accounts and those of the treasurer doing the best he could till the court could decide between them; (6) to look after "wafts, strays, goods lost, shipwrecks, whales, etc.," and get the country's part; (7) to keep a copy of all records of the court that concerned him; (8) to agree with colonial employees as to compensation, and see that the treasurer paid them; (9) to agree with state witnesses as to fees, and see about the expenses of patents, bounds, jurisdictions, etc.; (10) to see that the general and particular courts at Boston were provided for; (11) to do the same for the other courts of the colony, and draw on the treasurer for the bill; (12) to see to all other things touching the finances of the colony; (13) to sign no bill to be paid by the treasurer till he received his own pay.

§ 24. *The Laxity of Officials.*

That no permanent improvement resulted from the new arrangement is evident from the scattered entries relating to the treasurer and his accounts. Having appointed an auditor to look after the treasurer, the next thing for the court was to appoint a committee to look after the auditor. On October 7th, 1646, a committee was appointed to inquire into the conduct of constables, marshal, auditor and treasurer, and report eleven months later. On May 10th, 1648, it was ordered that the auditor general and Capt. Tyng take the treasurer's account once every year and present it to the general court, also the account of the present treasurer. On May 22nd, 1650, the court appointed another committee to take the treasurer's account, at the same time complaining that the previous committee had not done its work. That this committee really audited the treasurer's accounts, though no copy of its report is known to be in existence, is established by a reference to it in the report of a subsequent committee (January 20th, 1655). It is established by the same reference and borne out by other contemporary evidence,[1] that no further reports were made for the next five years, although at least two committees were appointed during the interval: the first, May 21st, 1652, being instructed to report at the next session; and the second, August 30th, 1653, including among its members the auditor general, being ordered to publish the gross sums, receipts and expenses.

§ 25. *The First Treasurer's Report.*

At last, however, twenty-eight years after the founding of the colony, and ten years after the commencement of a series

[1] "We intreate you will please to remember, that it is not long since there was more than an ordinary rate called for, * * but how it reached its end is best knowne to them, whoe had the disposing thereof, for wee never had any account thereof, which wee desire may be given to every town yeerely in perticulers."—Petition of Boston Freemen to General Court, September 1st, 1653. Original in Felt's Massachusetts Archives, Vol. 100, p. 44.

of repeated efforts by the general court, we have a report dated January 20th, 1655, made by a committee of the general court to the colonial secretary. It covers a period of four and a half years, and begins:

"Impr we find remayneing due fro the Country on the Ballance of the last accompt made in Septr 1650 unto severall psons then the sum of Sixteen hundred twentie and three pounds two shillings four penc ½ as it standeth one the Auditr Genr Booke."

The sources and amounts of receipts are as follows:

By half a year's rent wine license Oct., 1650.	£ 80
" four " " " " to Oct., 1654	£ 640
" two years' custom of wine in year 1653 and 1654 to Oct. @ £165 per annum	£ 330
" so much recd. of several other men for drawing wine which was not yearly rents	£ 79–13
" several fines Oct. 1650 to 20 Jan. 1654–'5	£ 255–19
" so much recd. by Court orders and petitions to Jan. 1654–'5.	£ 36–12
" 18 strings peage for Indian tribute @ 6 per d.	£ 45
" entry of actions to Jan. 1654	£ 100– 1– 6
	£1,567– 5– 6
" Rates recd. 1650.	£ 928–18– 0
" " " 1651.	£ 1455–17– 9
" " " 1652.	£ 1020– 2– 3
" " " 1653.	£ 1991–17–11
" " " 1654.	£ 1174– 0– 2½
Total	£ 8138– 1– 7½

The disbursements during the same time, added to the previous deficit, being £9237 17s. 0d., the committee find the present balance to be £1099 15s. 4½d. in favor of the treasurer.

§ 26. *Administrative Paralysis.*

In October, 1656, the auditor-general resigned his position; but he was prevailed upon to remain in office till the next session of the general court, when his resignation was accepted and the office abolished (October 23d, 1657). From this time on till the annulment of the colonial charter the organization of the financial administration remained the same as it had been at first; and the records show with tiresome continuity, the same inefficiency on the part of the treasurer in keeping accounts, the same neglect of duty on the part of auditing committees appointed from time to time, usually every two or three years, or when, as often happened from wars or other causes, the treasury was exhausted, and the same complaints, entreaties, threats and fruitless devices on the part of the court when its orders to treasurers and committees were disregarded. In 1665 the court began a determined campaign looking toward the production of the treasurer's accounts once more before them. October 11th, an auditing committee was appointed as usual; May 23d, 1666, the same committee, having as usual made no report, was continued and urged to bring in its report "as soon as the treasurer is ready;" October 9th, 1667, a new committee was appointed, and entreated to take the treasurer's account and report to the court; October 23d, 1668, the court grew emphatic, "ordering and enacting" that the committee then appointed do report forthwith; finally, November 7th, 1668, the last committee did make a report with great ceremony, having the governor attest it with his seal; and at the treasurer's request he and his heirs were forever discharged from any claims by the colony.[1] After this the pressure of the Dutch and Indian wars of the '70s brought out more frequent reports; but the same loose administrative methods prevailed in the main through the colonial period.[2]

[1] Original discharge filed in Felt's Massachusetts Archives, Vol. 100, p. 128.

[2] Here is the report of an auditing committee, of the later colonial period:

"In obedience to an order of ye Honored Genl Court, Dated May 19: *1680* Wee ye Subscribers met at the time Appointed to puse ye Country Treasurers Accompts, & accordingly proceeded Soo farr as we thought necessary unless long time be given for Examining it in ye pticulers, ye Accots being very Voluminious Comprised in ffower Large Leagors, But soo farr as wee Examined, And upon concideracon of ye whole doo judge ye Accots to be just, & Capt. Hull & Capt.

§ 27. *A Treasurer's Troubles.*

That the trouble about these records was not all due to the reluctance or inability of treasurers to make reports is plain from the following petition, the original of which will be found in Felt's Massachusetts Archives.[1]

To the Hono^ble^ Genrall Court Sitting in Boston, 7th Novemb^r^ 1683.

The Petition of Judith Hull & Samuel Sewall Administrt^rs^ of the Estate of the late John Hull Esqr sometime Treasurer dec^d^

Humbly Sheweth,

That whilst the s^d^ m^r^ Hull served the Country in ye Office or Imploy, as Treasurer for the warr and Treasurer of the Country hee did in the respective years from Septr 1678, to October, 1680, draw up sevrall accompts of Ballance in order to the passing his accomp^t^ that by reason of the other weighty affaires of the Country was deferred from Court to Court, untill the s^d^ accompt hath amounted to a very great sum, of which hee could not obtain a settlement in his life time:

How faithfully hee approved himselfe and ready to serve the Country both with his Estate and in person, is well known tomany, and labored under the weight of the accompt with his own hand, untill weakness of body and the bulke thereof necessitated him to take in Captn Daniel Henchman to his assistance, the accompt being of such nature and so vast, as could not be carried on but by keeping accompt of Species (there being above twelve thousand debendures orders and other acco^ts^

Henchman makeing oath thereto may be allowed by the honored Court, the Ballance due to ye Treasur^r^ p said Acco^t^ is Seaventeen hundred Seaventy three pounds & eleven pence money, the Said Treasur^r^ informes y^t^ Seaverall townes are in Arreares for their Rates, though Credit be given for ye whole, As also there is one hundred twenty Six pounds Eighteen Shillings four pence due to ye Country for ffines, captures, etc. We finde Capt Hull hath charged fifty two pounds p Annum for ffower years, as Capt Henchmans Salary for keeping ye Bookes but nothing for him selfe + Servants All wch wee psent to this Honored Court Dated in Boston, October ye 21th 1680."—Original report in Felt's Massachusetts Archives, Vol. 100, p. 257. To this report the magistrates agreed, but the deputies non-concurred.

[1] Vol. 100, p. 317

and papers filed) and besides by his paines, one of his Relations and two of his Apprentices did labour much in his Service for all of which he hath not charged one penny. That hee was all along many hundred pounds out of his own Estate for the supply of the Country in their streights by reason of danger at home, and occasions of Agency in England, and did preserve their Credit, by his takeing up and engageing for considerable Sumes on their behalfe, besides his own disburs'^{ts} to the lessening of his trade as is apparent.

"Hee hath given the Country credit for all their rates, though much standing out to this day, and no effectuall way for the gathering them in without trouble and charge; By his last Account hee had above Seventeen hundred pounds due to him from the Country, and charged but £425 : 15 : 4 interest for his own disburs'ts and long forbearance, wch if it had been many hundred more would not have compensated his damage: What hee hath received of m^{r} Russell, wch went to pay debts, there being great sumes oweing by the Country, is in an account supplementall to the last herewth presented, and therein incerted w^{t} erro^{rs} have been found by those Gentlem^{n} appointed to examine the same; as also by m^{r} Henchman, there being as well under as over charg^{d} some acco^{tts} misplaced, and some debts to persons wch are found not payable by the country, but the county of Yorke. There is also an additional accompt, drawing up of what receipts and paym^{ts} have been since the accompt given in wch will shortly be made up.

"The premisses considered yor Pet. Humbly Pray that this Hono^{ble} Court would please to order the passing s^{d} accompts, that transaction of so great a Sume as £52500 may not lye unsetled, and to take effectuall care for payment of the balance.

"And as in duty bound yor Pet^{rs} shall pray &c

"SAMUEL SEWALL."[1]

§ 28. *Currency and Banking.*

The inconvenience of making exchanges by barter, even to the slight extent of providing themselves with such necessar-

[1] Hull's accounts were finally inspected and a balance of £545, 3s, 10d $\frac{2}{4}$, found due him by the committee, November 27th, 1683, and ordered paid by the General Court. See documents in Massachusetts Archives, Vol. 100, p. 319 *et seq.*

ies of life as they did not individually produce, was early felt by the colonists in Massachusetts. Like the planters of most of the Anglo-American colonies, they had declared that the desire to convert the Indians to Christianity was their chief reason for coming to America. But they soon lost sight of this purpose; and when they found themselves driving a brisk and profitable trade with the savages, as well as developing considerable commerce among themselves, they turned anxiously to the consideration of the question of currency. Wampumpeage and beaver-skin money, even when added to the scanty supply of English and Spanish coin which the early colonists possessed, and which was continually flowing away from them in exchange for commodities of European manufacture, served but poorly to eke out the circulating medium to a quantity barely sufficient for the commercial needs of the community. It is known that as early as 1652 the general court of Massachusetts was considering "all sorts of trading," and "the best ways of improving the same;"[1] that the questions relating to "raiseing a *Banke*,"[2] and to "monies in regard to the badnesse of it, or highnesse or lownesse of it, with very many other matters tending to the promoting and well regulating of trade"[2] had been discussed without and within the legislature; and that about the same time "for some years paper bills passed for payment of debts."[2] "Under what association or on what security these bills were issued, does not appear. The establishment of a mint, May, 1652, probably put a stop for a time to any movement towards 'raising a bank.' The author of 'Severals relating to the Fund' alludes to some such movement, but 'before anything was brought to effect,' he 'was called to Ireland,' and discontinued his endeavors to promote the banking project."[3]

[1] Massachusetts Records, III., 267; IV., Pt. 1, 86.

[2] Massachusetts Archives, quoted by Felt, Massachusetts Currency, 33.

[3] Trumbull, First Essays at Banking, 7–8.

§ 29. *The Colonial Mint.*

The history of the Massachusetts colonial mint is too well known to require repetition here. It is easy from the vantage ground of our present knowledge of the science of finance to point out mistakes in the details of the management of this unique institution in American colonial history.[1] The unscientific shape and finish of the Massachusetts coins, especially the earlier ones,[2] and the extravagance of the contracts with Mintmaster Hull,[3] are legitimate subjects for criticism; and the policy of undervaluation as compared with the English standard,[4] while prompted by an intelligible motive, could only work to the disadvantage of the colony in the end. Yet justice requires us to declare that the mint on the whole was of immense advantage to the colony. Established at a time

[1] Chalmers says that Maryland had a mint in 1662; but Thomas Hutchinson, afterward governor of Massachusetts, writing of a New England shilling and sixpence which he was sending as curiosities to a correspondent in England, in February, 1761, says "no other colony ever had any coin." Quoted by Felt, Massachusetts Currency, p. 49, n.

[2] "For forme flatt and square on the sides, and stamped on the one side with *NE*, and on the other side, with the figure XIId, VId, and IIId, according to the valew of each peece, together with a privy marke, which shall be appointed euery three months by the Gouernor, and knowne only to him and the sworne officers of the mint." Massachusetts Records, May 31st, 1652, quoted by Felt, Massachusetts Currency, p. 31.

[3] In 1652, "The mint master, for himselfe and officers, for their paynes and labour in melting and refining and coyning, is allowed to take one shilling out of every twenty shillings which he shall stampe."—*Ibid.* And in 1675, "fiueteen pence in the whole for euery twenty shillings, and the said minters to pay into the Treasury of the Country in money twenty pounds per ann."—*Ibid.*, p. 42.

[4] "The sayd master of the mint aforesaid is hereby required to coyne all the said money of good silver of the just alloy of new starling English money, and for valew to stampe two pence in a shilling of less valew than the present English coyne, and the lesser peeces proportionably."—Massachusetts Records, act of May 31st, 1652, quoted by Felt, Massachusetts Currency, 31. Maryland decides "that their coin, issued from such an establishment, shall be equivalent to English sterling."—Felt, Massachusetts Currency, p. 38, apparently on the strength of an assertion of Chalmers.

when the overthrow of the traditional form of government in England had seemed to render uncertain the continuance of the colonial relation between the mother country and the most independent of all her children, and maintained in the face of repeated and unmistakable expressions of royal displeasure, for more than a third of a century the mint served a most useful purpose in the colony by furnishing the inhabitants with a stable, if somewhat depreciated, currency. It fell in the fall of the colonial charter, with the continuance of which the revival of the mint had come to be inseparably associated in the royal mind; but its salutary financial influence was felt in the colony and in New England as long as the rude but honest product of its operation circulated in the channels of trade.[1]

§ 30. *Woodbridge's Bank.*

Even while the mint, operated in the face of the king's displeasure, was pouring forth its slender but constant stream of New England shillings and six-pences,[2] various projects arose for reënforcing the circulating medium of the colonies by the establishment of banks for issuing paper money.[3] An attempt made in 1664, by the author of "Severals relating to the Fund"—the Rev. John Woodbridge, if we may accept the conclusion of so distinguished an antiquarian as Dr. J. Hammond Trumbull—to interest influential merchants in a plan which he had long had in mind[4] for "a way of trade & banke without money," is known to have been without practical result. A draught of his scheme in the shape of a "Proposal" pre-

[1] "However the mint was thus absolutely terminated, yet the products of its operation were long current in our country. Down to the Revolution of our Independence, they were often seen, and passed readily in business transactions, with other coin.'—Felt, Massachusetts Currency, 49.

[2] The coinage of threepences was not long continued.

[3] For some account of a scheme of Gov. John Winthrop, of Connecticut, for such a bank, see Trumbull, First Essays in Banking, 8–9.

[4] Since 1650. See Severals relating to the Fund.

sented by the author to the colonial council "about three years after this" and embodied in "Severals relating to the Fund," reveals the nature of the project. It is entitled: "A Proposal for erecting a FUND of *Land*, by Authority, or Private Persons, in the nature of a *Money-Bank;* or *Merchandise-Lumber*, to pass Credit upon, by *Book-Entries;* or *Bils of* Exchange, for great Payments; and *Charge-bills* for running Cash. Wherein is demonstrated, First, the necessity of having a *Bank*, to enlarge the *Measure* of Dealings in this Land, by shewing the benefit of *Money*, if enough to mete Trade with; and the disadvantages, when it is otherwise;" and "Secondly, That Credit pass'd in *Fund*, by Book, and Bills (as afore) will fully supply the defect of *Money*. Wherein is related, of how little value *Coin*, as the Measure of Trade, need be, in itself; what Inconveniencies subject to. The worth a *Fund*-Bill, or Payment therein, is of: & not of that Hazard."[1] The author's "narrative" of how the plan was put into practice is wanting in the only copy of "Severals relating to the Fund" which is known to have been preserved.[2] "Enough remains, however," says Doctor Trumbull, "to establish the facts, that a 'Fund of Land' or bank of credit was started in Massachusetts in March, 1671, and was 'carried on in private for many months'—though without issue of bills, and that, ten years later, a private bank of credit was established and began to issue bills in September, 1681. Of the result of this enterprise we have no information—except in the assurance that it did not ruin its projectors."[3]

§ 31. *Blackwell's Bank.*

Five years after the date last mentioned, John Blackwell, of Boston, "on behalf of himselfe and divers others, his participants, as well in England as in this Countrey," laid before President Dudley and his council a proposal and "Constitution,

[1] Quoted by Trumbull, First Essays, 10.

[2] See Bibliography.

[3] First Essays, 12.

Modell Frame of Rules and Orders requisit, and to be observed, in the erecting and maintaining of a Bank of Credit Lumbard and Exchange of Moneys by Persons of approved Integrity, prudence & estates in this Country, wherein such a foundation is layd for delivering out Bills, or giving Credit, on such Real Estates of Lands, as also personal Estates of goods and Merchandizes not subject to perishing or decay." Blackwell had been treasurer of the army under Cromwell, and after his arrival in Boston in 1684, commissioned by "divers persons in England and Ireland, gentlemen, citizens, and others, being 'inclined to remove themselves into foreign parts," had become intimate with Dudley. His proposal and constitution having been reported upon favorably by "the Grand and Standing Committee, consisting of divers eminent & worthy persons, Merchants and others," to whom it had been referred, the president and council on September 27th, 1686, judging "the said undertaking is not only lawfull to be managed by any of his Majesties subjects, as any other calling, but will tend much to his Majesties service, and the benefit of these parts," "do therefore * * * own the sayd proposall as a publique and useful invention for this Countrey," and "thinke fitt in his Majesties name to declare our Approbation, Allowance, and Recomendation thereof."[1] All that has thus far been ascertained concerning this association, the first chartered bank in Massachusetts, is contained in a brief reference to it made by the anonymous writer of a rare pamphlet printed in 1714:

"Our Fathers about Twenty-eight years ago, entered into a Partnership to circulate their Notes founded on Land Security, stamped on Paper, as our Province Bills, which gave no offence to the Government then," etc.[2]

[1] Original in Felt's Massachusetts Archives, Vol. 126, pp. 104–'7.

[2] Quoted by Felt, Massachusetts Currency, 47, from Boston Athenæum Tracts, C. 121, and by Trumbull, First Essays, 14, from "Letter from one in Boston to his Friend in the Country, in answer to a Letter to John Burrill Esq. Speaker to the House of Representatives, for the Province of Massachusetts Bay in New-England," Boston, 1714, pp. 37.

Dr. Trumbull believes that it did not survive the presidency of Dudley, as Blackwell, the prime mover of the enterprise, left Boston with a commission from William Penn, as governor of Pennsylvania, in November, 1688, and did not return till 1690, before the end of which year the colony of Massachusetts took to itself the office and obligations of a "bank of credit."[1]

§ 32. *The Colonial Finances.*

What, now, was the financial condition of the colony under the system the development of which has been described? When, after seven years of struggle and privation, the victory over the stubborn forces of nature upon an inhospitable shore was fairly won; when the land, under careful tillage, began to produce more than was sufficient to support the inhabitants in comfort; and commerce with the West Indies, the wine islands, the southern American colonies and with England began to spring up: with a financial system providing for a revenue from both static and dynamic taxation—did the colonists begin to realize in their growing commonwealth the blessings of financial independence and stability? Nothing is more certain than the answer to this question. It must be confessed that not only during those earliest years when the colony, like ancient Rome in the first period of her history, was struggling for existence, but all through the period of the colonial charter, through the period of the provincial charter, through the period of the continental revolution, Massachusetts was convulsed with financial crises whose magnitude increased with the growth of the commonwealth and whose frequency did not diminish in an equal ratio. With the inexhaustible resources of a virgin soil, of waters teeming with fish, of forests filled with game, with all the useful and valuable, though for the most part raw, materials of a constantly developing country at hand, and with neither civil nor ecclesiastical tyrants to hamper the growth of the commonwealth, the colony was yet

[1] Trumbull, First Essays, 14.

destitute of those reserves of material force—the result of a financial system well developed and well administered—which have enabled states poorer than Massachusetts was to withstand successfully severer financial strains than she was ever called upon to endure.

§ 33. *Causes of Instability.*

The chief causes of this instability of fortune which was particularly characteristic of the colonial period are not far to seek. They were not the poverty of the richest colony in New England, not the inadequacy of the best tax system in America. They were, first, the improvidence of the people, as reflected in the financial legislation of their representatives; secondly, the weakness and irresolution of the financial administration; and thirdly, the custom of receiving "specie" in payment of taxes.

It was doubtless the fear of encouraging in however slight a degree the establishment of centralized and irresponsible power such as that from the exercise of which the colonists suffered in the mother-country, that dictated the hesitating, hand-to-mouth policy displayed in all the colonial and provincial legislation, but especially in the laws pertaining to taxation. The practical disadvantages of such a course were felt in many ways, not only in Massachusetts but in England, where, at a later period, the lords of trade objected to it as highly embarrassing to both countries. The effect of the practice upon the condition of the colonial treasury was particularly bad, as it encouraged the people to put off the payment of taxes; hoping, like Mr. Micawber, that something would turn up to do away with the necessity of paying them at all.

The conflict in the minds of the early legislators between the desire on the one hand to make the tax system effective, and the temptation on the other to yield to solicitations for exemptions, to which a recent writer has called attention as characteristic of the legislation of New York in the eighteenth century,[1] is no less obvious in the financial legislation of Massachusetts in the seventeenth. The frequency with which these requests from towns, parishes and individuals were granted, between the loss of the sums directly remitted and the losses entailed through delays on the part of taxpayers, which like the policy above mentioned, it did much to encourage, resulted in large depletions of the public revenues.

§ 34. "*Specie*" *Payments.*

If anything more was needed to minimize the results obtained under the colonial system of taxation, it was found in the custom of receiving "specie" for taxes, which prevailed from the earliest times. By "specie" or "country pay" was meant whatever kind of produce or even live stock the taxpayer had to offer. The embarrassments experienced in the practical operation of a financial system in which the medium of payment was subject to material diminutions in value early led to the repeal of the law authorizing the experiment of allowing taxes to be paid in wampum. That the infinitely more troublesome and wasteful custom of permitting the payment of taxes to be made in "specie" was tolerated long afterward, is without doubt principally due to the reluctance on the part of the colonial legislators to discommode individual constituents, of which mention has already been made. The effect of its continuance upon the treasury was in every way disastrous. From the moment the taxpayer unloaded his "specie" upon the constable until the treasurer actually had in his hand the money ultimately realized from the sale of it, there was nothing but a succession of deteriorations and

[1] "The tax legislation of the last century was characterized on the one hand by a desire to make the existing tax system more effective, and on the other hand by the anxiety it displayed not to hurt the feelings of the tax-payer."—Schwab, History of the New York Property Tax, 60.

losses.[1] From the scanty figures preserved in the treasurer's records, it appears that from January 1st, 1689, to April 17th, 1689, a period of three and one-half months, the losses to the treasury from the sale of 9,977¾ bushels of grain were no less than £99 1s 3d, or a rate of nearly £400 per year.

§ 35. *The "Usurpation."*

The six years intervening between the nullification of the first charter of Massachusetts Bay[2] and the granting of the second[3] were years of political violence in New England, and the few financial records of the period that have been preserved are scattered and fragmentary. But the treatment which the colonists received at the hands of Dudley, and especially at

[1] See representation of John Pynchon to the General Court as to the loss of a cargo of peas in the Connecticut river, sent for taxes to Springfield, Felt's Massachusetts Archives, Vol. 100, p. 441. Also

"An Accompt of Damages Sustained by Eleazer Gyles and Abraham Cole late Constables of Salem at the time of the Indian Warr Anno 1676 in the coelecting and paying out of the Rates by them received—being 16 Single Country-Rates Amg to about £1200.

Imp By loss of measure in the severall graines recd by us, about 80 bushells £15–00–00

By loss in the fall of the price from the time of or collecting unto or paying it out again by bills drawn upon us from the Tr the warrants ordering in the first ten rates to receive Indian at 3/6, wheat at 6/8 and so proportionable, and wee could not put it off again, for payment of the Trs bills but at 18d, 20d and sometimes 21d for Indian, and wheate 5d per bushll wee judge or loss could not amo to less then £38–00–00

By payment of Storage for grain [thus?] lying in or hands neer two years £10–00–00

£63–00–00."

The magistrates agreed to abate the petitioners £30, but the deputies "consented not." See the original in Felt's Massassachusetts Archives, Vol. 100, p. 259.

[2] June 18th, 1684.

[3] 1690.

the hands of Andros, was not such as easily to have been overlooked by those who suffered from it, nor forgotten by those who came after them. The royal commission to Sir Edmund Andros as Governor-General of New England[1] gave him authority, by the consent of a council appointed by himself and removable at his pleasure, "to impose, and assess, and raise, and levy, such rates and taxes as you shall find necessary for the support of the government."[2] An order of March 3rd, 1687, the text of which has been preserved, signed by Andros in the teeth of the opposition of his council, shows that the Governor-General retained the method of assessment by a commissioner in each town acting with the selectmen, as well as the other main features of the tax system which he found in operation in Massachusetts. The expenses of Andros's government are stated by Hutchinson not to have been excessive; it was against what the colonists regarded as the exercise of power usurped, not alone in his sitting in the governor's chair at all without the charter, but in his utter disregard of the expressed will of his own council,[3] rather than against the amount of the financial burdens imposed by him, that they so vigorously, though ineffectually, protested in 1687. The greatly increased expenses of the government during the second year of his administration, due to the outbreak of a war with the Indians, were more willingly allowed by the council and borne by the people in the presence of the common foe.

§ 36. *An Interesting Document.*

The most interesting financial document of this period that has come down to us is a mere fragment of a report, showing that while the seventeen hundred polls over sixteen years of age, in Boston, in 1688, were assessed, at the rate of twenty

[1] 1686.

[2] Felt, Statistics.

[3] Felt, Statistics, 264.

pence each, an aggregate of £124. 18s. 4d., the rateable estates of the town for the same year, assessed at the rate of one penny per pound, yielded no more than £83, 4s, 8¼d. We know not whether the above figures represent the state of affairs existing in the other towns of the colony; nor can it now be ascertained to how great an extent the undervaluation of property by the assessors was carried, in view of the unpopularity of Andros's government. But when the people of a community are subjected, whether by an authority legally or illegally constituted, to a poll tax which is, in any event, nearly fifty per cent. greater than the tax upon property, it is certainly time that a new financial régime be inaugurated in that community. Add to this the enormous fees exacted by the government for all ministerial services,—the fee for the probating of wills, for example, being no less than fifty shillings, in addition to the expenses of a journey to Boston, while that for confirming patents of lands issued under the charter, and now declared void by Andros, on the ground that the charter itself had been nullified, amounted in some instances to fifty pounds, and it would seem that the measure of administrative iniquity was filled up.

§ 37. *The Downfall of Andros.*

Not all the astuteness manifested by Andros in graduating his patent-fees according to time and circumstances and people and estates could screen him from the accumulating wrath of the colonists in his attempts to extort from them a sum so great that, according to a computation made at the time, not all the personal property in the colony would have been sufficient to pay it had the charges for all the new patents been made at one time. The accession of William and Mary to the throne of England was the signal for the seizure and imprisonment of Andros and his lieutenants and the re-establishment[1] of the charter government; but the people of

[1] June 22nd, 1689.

the colony had hardly had time to manifest their satisfaction at the overthrow of their oppressor, by cheerfully voting twenty rates[1] (a much larger number than had ever before been voted at a single time) to defray the expenses of the Indian war and by other acts of self-denial, when the arrival of a new charter[2], uniting under a single government the colonies of Massachusetts Bay and Plymouth, together with Maine, Nova Scotia and other vast tracts of territory to the north, inaugurated a new financial, as well as political era in the history of what now became the province of Massachusetts Bay.

§ 38. *Condition of the Finances.*

The unexpectedness of Sir Edmund's involuntary withdrawal from the country may be accepted, in his behalf, as a sufficient explanation of the confused condition in which the public accounts were left by that event. Among those features of the Massachusetts system with which he saw no reason to interfere, upon assuming the government, was the custom of permitting the colonial treasurer to advance to the government as much money as he was able and willing to spare, and to wait for reimbursement till the general court should order a tax. When Treasurer Usher, through this process, reached the bottom of his purse, Sir Edmund drew further supplies from the merchants of Boston and others, issuing upon his own official responsibility debentures for the amounts so obtained. Both these practices entailed considerable trouble upon the new government after Andros's downfall.[3] The court made no objection to the payment of the debentures

[1] November 7th, 1690

[2] 1692.

[3] For an example of the good number of petitions that were presented to the general court for payment of the Andros debentures, see the one dated January 14th, 1693, in Felt's Massachusetts Archives, Vol. 100, p. 452, from seven inhabitants of Boston, merchants and others, for the payment of debentures given by the late government for money lent, and vessels and other property impressed for service against the French and Indians.

where it was plain that the supplies for which they had been given had been used in the defense of the country.[1] There was, however, less promptness in allowing the late treasurer's accounts,[2] concerning the settlement of which no little corres-

[1] In 1701 the report of a committee appointed in July, 1699, and since then several times continued, to settle up and issue debentures for the debts incurred by Andros, gave the aggregate of such debts as £5882 0s. 11d. Felt's Massachusetts Archives, Vol. 101, p. 214.

[2] On March 22d, 1693–4, a committee of the council appointed to examine the accounts of the late governor, Sir Edmund Andros, and the late treasurer, John Usher, "Referred by order from the Rt Honble the Lords of their Majtys most Honble Privy Council, unto the Examinacōn" of the governor and company of Massachusetts Bay, reported that they had inspected the accounts presented by Usher, beginning May 25th, 1686, in the time of the president and council, and ending July 1st, 1690; that they found due Usher £851 2s. 10d.; and that they found "standing out" of the several rates then made £798 17s. 3d. beside £27 9s. outlawed by time. Upon consideration of this report, and a further examination of the accounts of Usher, exceptions were taken to the following items in the account: First, to £4,286 9s. 4d. salary to Andros "the moneys so applied being drawn out of the treasury by his own orders, no advice and consent of the Council appearing for ye same." Secondly, to the charge of 5 per cent. commission on the salary of the treasurer, amounting to £700 or upwards, "there appearing no order of the Governor and Council for allowing of the same."—See Felt's Massachusetts Archives, Vol. 101, pp. 1, 2, where also Usher's accounts, apparently in his own hand, are given *in extenso*. A year later, "his majesty's command given at the council chamber at Whitehall, 26 March 1694, to proceed to a final examination of the accounts" of Usher "and satisfy him out of the public stock, for the balance due him for his account pursuant to an order in council of 12 October 1691, or else to return an account of their proceedings and their reasons for not having complied," produced no other result than a restatement of the former objections to the items of Andros's salary and his percentage upon that of the treasurer, to which was now added the claim for £683 11s. 6d. for the surveyor and auditor general. "As to the Minute of Council relating to Sr Edmd Andros's Salary, dated ye 17th of March 1688," says the draught of this paper contained in Felt's Massachusetts Archives, Vol. 101, pp. 11–14, "[it] mentions no Sum in gross, nor what his Salary is per anno, no time when it commences, nor any waies directs how either of them may be ascertained; but is Entered onely in these words that is to say Ordered, That the Treasurer do Satisfy his Excy, for his Salary out of his Majtys Revenue till Xmas last past. Yet the account is charged with £750 as paid for one year's salary five days after his arrival in the Government, and £750 at the end of each half year for one year following." The paper also objects to certain items as not belonging properly to

pondence between the new government and the lords of the English privy council was found to be necessary.

the province to pay, to mistakes in the reckoning of time, and to the addition of 25 per cent. to make the account sterling. There is another and neater though less legible draught of this document in Felt's Massachusetts Archives, Vol. 101, pp. 18–19, which advances still other objections; but this draught has no signatures. On March 17th, 1702–3, a report of a committee on John Usher's petition allowed him £187 15s. 5d.; but there was a non-concurrence. On June 27th, 1702, upon petition of David Jefferies, attorney for John Usher, another committee was appointed to go over the whole matter and all the records again.

BOOK II.

THE PROVINCE OF MASSACHUSETTS BAY.

§ 39. *Opposition to the New Charter.*

At no period in the history of Massachusetts has the vital relation that exists between the political and the financial life of a community been more clearly shown than in the years of financial perturbation that followed the reorganization of the government under the provincial charter. Through more than sixty years of alternate neglect and interference, the colonists had learned to take substantial advantage of the vagueness of the provisions of King James's charter, to the increasing impairment of the royal prerogative. The new instrument, while it sextupled the territory of the colony and greatly augmented its resources and importance, yet, in the matters of the appointment of the governor, the constitution of the legislature and the reservation of the veto power, made it far more dependent than before upon the royal will. At the same time it greatly increased the responsibility and the difficulty of administering the government. The dissatisfaction of the people at the refusal of the new king and queen to tolerate a continuance of the old order of things was much more general and intense than historians have realized.[1] It is here that we are to look for the beginnings of that feeling of separation

[1] "There is a general buzzing among the people, great with expectation of their old charter or they know not what; such was the ominous message of Andros to Brockholst, with orders that the soldiers should be ready for action."—Bancroft's History of the United States, Edition of 1882, I., 599. "Of fifty-four towns, forty certainly, probably more, voted to reassume the old charter. Representatives were chosen, and, on the 22d of May, Massachusetts once more assembled in general court."—*Ibid.*, I., 600.

between the people and the government which showed itself throughout the provincial period, partly in a growing jealousy on the part of the popular branch of the legislature, with reference to the policy of the governor and his council, partly in the reluctance of the people to obey many of the laws, especially those relating to the raising or expenditure of moneys, which they believed were made in the king's interest rather than in their own, and partly in the origination of a large amount of automatic legislation, by which it was fondly believed that laws repugnant to the public sense could be made to execute themselves. Combining with other influences, it ended only with that disturbance of political relations with the mother country known in history as the American Revolution.[1]

§ 40. *The Charter goes into Effect.*

But the new charter had come, and it had come to stay: they must accept it in good faith, and do the best they could with it. The king in a spirit of conciliation appointed to be the first provincial governor Sir William Phips, a native of New England, and a soldier who had greatly endeared himself to the people of Massachusetts as commander of their troops in the late war with the French. Moreover, the condition of the country at the moment was one calling for united effort. As in the days of Andros the common danger of an Indian war had constrained the people to support the government in spite of their abhorrence of the man, so now a combination of conditions unfavorable to any violent manifestation of dissatisfaction—the emptiness of the colonial treasury, the embarrassment of almost continuous Indian wars lasting down to 1714 and finally the great fire of Boston in 1711—led them to forget, or at least to overlook those objectionable features of the charter which in more prosperous times they would have erected into mountains of difficulty, and upon which,

[1] Cf. Felt, History of Massachusetts Currency.

indeed, as after events too plainly showed, they had good reason to look with a suspicious eye. The organization of the government under the new charter meant the expansion, the systemization and the invigoration of all its functions. Above all, it meant a great increase in public expenditures and the creation, upon principles of equity and economy, of a correspondingly augmented revenue, all but an infinitesimal portion of which must come from the people themselves. Such was the financial problem that confronted the new government; to its solution they gave their immediate and earnest attention.

CHAPTER I.

DIRECT TAXATION.

§41. *Early Provincial Legislation.*

As soon as the new provincial legislature had provided against the interruption of the business of the community by continuing all the local laws of the late colonies of Massachusetts Bay and New Plymouth that were not repugnant to the laws of England nor inconsistent with the provisions of the provincial charter, they turned their attention to financial matters; and of the nine other acts—all important—passed by them at their first session no fewer than five were purely financial. There were arrears of "public assessments," as well as of "town and county rates," levied by the late governments; and for the collection of these two special acts were passed. The fourth act of the session grants to their majesties an assessment upon polls and estates; and the fifth an impost, excise and tonnage upon shipping; while another prolongs the life of the bills of credit issued by the late colony of Massachusetts Bay. It is with the history of direct taxation in the province that we are first concerned.

The brief but important tax act of June 24th–July 2d, 1692,[1] contains but two variations, neither of them important, from the forms with which we are already familiar as characteristic of the tax system of Massachusetts Bay for the fifty years of its history immediately preceding the Andros period. The class exempted from the payment of the poll tax was enlarged so as to include not only settled ministers and grammar-

[1] 1692–'3, c. 5.

school masters, but also members of the council, all persons devoted to the ministry and students of the college; and the property tax was assessed in the form of a large proportion—twenty-five per cent.—of one year's income from all personal and real estate. The act may thus be taken as an epitome of the colonial system of taxation. But the promise that seemed to be held out by its passage, of a continuity of financial activity, was far from being fulfilled in the history of the next few years.

§ 42. *Failure and Reform.*

It was due undoubtedly to the causes above mentioned,[1] rather than to any failure on the part of the tax officers or of the people to understand the provisions of the simple act of June 24th–July 2nd, 1692[2]—an excuse which the government, however, kindly advanced for them—that the act proved so great a failure in execution under the new conditions. The following December a supplementary act was passed, four times as long as the previous one, and full of minute provisions, some of them extraordinary ones, for reassessing and collecting the former tax, together with an additional sum made necessary by the embarrassment in which the government now found itself. Thus the first tax act under the new charter, instead of becoming, as its framers doubtless expected it would, the opening act of a new financial epoch, proved to be the closing act of an old one. The great trouble lay with the assessors, who very generally throughout the province either altogether neglected to make the assessments, or else made them so unevenly that widespread dissatisfaction was the result. The returns to the treasury were wholly inadequate.

It was, more than anything else, to bring this recalcitrant class of officials to a sense of duty that the multifarious and radical changes in the forms of the next seven tax acts were made. Assessors separate from the selectmen, town commis-

[1] § 39.

[2] 1692–'3, c. 5.

missioners for county equalization, county commissioners for provincial equalization, county and town apportionment by the general court, oaths for the assessors, property qualifications for the assessors, penalties upon the towns for not electing assessors, penalties upon assessors for not serving when elected, provisions for the election of new assessors in case of death or failure to act, powers to require lists of property from inhabitants, penalties upon inhabitants for not furnishing such lists, duties of the assessors minutely defined, classes of real property enumerated, classes of personal property enumerated and specifically rated, allowance to assessors for time and trouble, solemn injunctions upon towns, assessors and collectors to perform their duties, frantic omnibus sections conferring upon everybody all the powers ever conferred upon anybody and pronouncing upon everybody all the penalties ever pronounced upon anybody—such are some of the expedients which the government was constrained to adopt in quick succession in order to supply the treasury with funds by the taxation of an indifferent, if not unwilling, people, and most of which it as quickly abandoned as being partially or wholly inadequate to that end.

§ 43. *The Turning Point.*

The act of June 27th, 1695–6,[1] may be taken as marking the turning point of this crudely experimental legislation. Beginning with the act of June 17th, 1696,[2] eight successive tax acts show but little variation till in the general act of March 20th, 1699–1700,[3] the legislature committed the province for a period of three years in advance to a system which is thus shown to have worked with reasonable success. This act was revived bodily from time to time, for periods varying from one to eight years, until, by the general act of October

[1] 1695–'6, c. 6.

[2] 1696, c. 3.

[3] 1699–1700, c. 26.

3d, 1730,[1] the system was adopted without limit; and it remained without material change throughout the provincial period and well into the present century. The importance of this first decade of the second charter as the crystallizing period of Massachusetts tax legislation is quite likely to be overlooked, even in a careful examination of the different tax acts: it can be fully grasped only after an analysis of the completed system, and a tracing of the history of each of its component parts from its first appearance to its permanent formulation.

§ 44. *The Choice of Assessors.*

The principle upon which the choice of assessors in Massachusetts has rested, not only during the provincial period, but during the colonial and state periods as well, is that of direct popular suffrage in the respective towns. The appointment by the general court, in 1692–'3,[2] of county commissioners for equalizing the quotas of the towns, and the provisions of the special law of 1694–'5[3] and of the general laws of 1699–1700[4] and 1730[5] for the appointment of assessors by the justices of the county were exceptions in the nature of a last resort, the first to extricate the provincial finances from a pressing emergency, and the others to guard against the recurrence of such an emergency. The first financial reform effected under the second charter—and it was an important one—was the substitution of a fixed period of service for the assessors in place of the single levy of the colonial régime. Only two acts of this decade, the first and third tax acts (the second tax act being in reality a part of the first one) direct the treasurer to send out his warrants to the selectmen to call meetings of the voters in their respective towns for the election of a com-

[1] 1730, c. 1.

[2] 1692–'3, c. 41.

[3] 1694–'5, c. 2.

[4] 1699–1700, c. 26.

[5] 1730, c. 1.

missioner, in the first instance in each town to act temporarily in conjunction with the selectmen as a board of assessors, and in the second instance to elect a separate board of assessors for that tax. In the act of June 18th–20th, 1694–'5,[1] the assessors of the previous act are again employed; and, beginning with the next act, that of September 14th, 1694–'5,[2] the period has uniformly been one year.

§ 45. *Changes in the System.*

The election of town commissioners—an office inherited from the colony—to serve with the selectmen in making assessments and to act by themselves as a board of town equalization, was provided for in the tax acts of June 24th, 1692–'3,[3] and June 27th, 1695–'6;[4] but, after recognition as a part of the tax system by the act of March 7th, 1695–'6,[5] that official disappears forever. Meanwhile the act of November 16th, 1692–'3,[6] provided for the election of a committee for assessment in each town, at the annual town meeting in March, when other officers were elected.

The tax acts, from that of October 27th, 1694–5,[7] to that of July 14th, 1699–1700,[8] recognize the two systems, selectmen or trustees in certain towns and separate boards of assessors in others as existing side by side; though the act of June 17th, 1696,[9] is the only one during this interval that specifically authorizes the election of separate boards by towns that prefer

[1] 1694–'95, c. 2.

[2] 1694–'5, c. 12.

[3] 1692–'3, c. 4.

[4] 1695–'6, c. 6.

[5] 1695–'6, c. 17.

[6] 1692–'3, c. 28.

[7] 1694–'5, c. 16.

[8] 1699–1700, c. 14.

[9] 1696, c. 3.

them. With the famous act of March 20th, 1699–1700,[1] however, the dual system was placed on a permanent legal footing.

§ 46. *Number of Assessors; Time of Choice.*

By the important act of November 16th, 1692–3,[2] for "regulating the townships, choice of town officers, and setting forth their power," the number of selectmen for each town was fixed at three, five, seven or nine. The town commissioner acting with the selectmen, until the disappearance of that official, would make the number even. All acts authorizing or prescribing separate boards of assessors specify odd numbers—three, five, seven or nine—except those of June 18th–20th, 1694–5,[3] and March 20th, 1699–1700,[4] which say "three or more." Evidently the purpose in all these acts was to guard against inconveniences arising intentionally or unintentionally from tie votes.

As to times for choosing assessors, the acts of June 24th, 1692–3,[5] and June 27th, 1695–6,[6] direct the treasurer to issue his warrants forthwith for the selectmen in each town to call a town meeting to be held in July following. Other acts employ boards already existing; until the act of March 20th, 1699–1700,[4] provides for the election of assessors, in towns preferring separate boards, at the annual town meeting in March—a plan that continued throughout the provincial period.

§47. *Qualifications of Assessors.*

Coming now to the matter of the qualifications of assessors,

[1] 1699–1700, c. 26.

[2] 1692–'3, c. 28.

[3] 1694–'5, c. 2.

[4] 1699–1700, c. 26.

[5] 1692–'3, c. 4.

[6] 1695–'6, c. 6.

the act of November 16th, 1692–3,[1] above referred to, required the selectmen of each town to be "able and discreet, of good conversation, inhabitants within such town." The acts of June 24th, 1692–3,[2] and June 27th, 1695–6,[3] required town commissioners to be "freeholders." The evident purpose of the general court to include a captain of militia in every pair of county commissioners provided for by the supplementary act of December 15th, 1692–3,[4] was carried out in the case of every county except York, the court itself naming the commissioners. In no particular is the radical nature of the tax legislation of 1694–5[5] more plainly shown than in the qualifications which it requires in the members of its separate board of assessors. The conventional qualifications of ability, discretion, good conversation and residence were given a decidedly practical turn by the requirement that every assessor be a freeholder reputed to be worth, in the case of towns of less than forty thousand inhabitants, not less than fifty pounds sterling, in the case of other towns, not less than one hundred, and in the case of Boston, not less than three hundred. The full significance of this requirement will be seen in connection with our discussion of penalties. In this, as in other particulars, the act of June 18th–20th, 1694–5,[5] went too far. After the next act, which employed the old assessors, all property qualifications dropped out of sight till the act of June 17th, 1696,[6] which merely required assessors to be freeholders in their respective towns or precincts. After this not only did all property qualifications disappear, but no qualifications whatever were specified. Finally the fundamental act of March 20th, 1699–1700,[7] again

[1] 1692–'3, c. 28.

[2] 1692–'3, c. 4.

[3] 1695–'6, c. 6.

[4] 1692–'3, c. 41.

[5] 1694–'5, c. 2.

[6] 1696, c. 3.

[7] 1699–1700, c. 26.

exacted residence, as did that of October 3rd,–7th, 1730,[1] in which condition the matter rested.

§ 48. *Assessors' Oaths.*

Another innovation of June 18th–20th, 1694–5,[2] aimed at the derelict assessors, was the requirement of an assessors' oath, a feature which, although it was omitted from the mildly reactionary law of October 27th, 1694–5, was revived by the act of June 17th, 1696; and ever since that time it has remained an essential feature of the Massachusetts system. The continual variation in the phraseology of the oaths, though doubtless good evidence of efforts on the part of successive legislatures to goad the assessors to a stricter performance of duty, as similar variations in the form of assesors' oaths in other colonies may be,[3] can hardly have accomplished much in that direction, since they really added nothing to the original oath —a promise before God to lay assessments impartially and acording to law. The weakness of the act of June 18th–20th, 1694–5,[4] in making no provision as to when, where or before whom the oath should be taken, was partially remedied when the law of June 17th, 1696,[5] provided that the oath should be taken before a justice of the peace, or the town clerk in towns where no justice resided; and it was entirely removed by a clause in the laws of March 20th, 1699–1700,[6] and October 3rd–7th, 1730,[7] directing the town clerk or one or two of the selectmen of every town, immediately on the election of assessors, to provide the constable or constables of the same with a list of those chosen to be assessors in their respective towns,

[1] 1730, c. 1.

[2] 1694–'5, c. 2.

[3] Schwab, History New York Property Tax, 60; Worthington, Finances of Pennsylvania, 78.

[4] 1694–'5, c. 2.

[5] 1696, c. 3.

[6] 1699–1700, c. 26.

[7] 1730, c. 1.

the constables being required "thereupon to summon each of the said assessors to appear at a certain time and place within the space of seven days from the day of their election, before a justice of the peace, if any dwell in such town, or otherwise before the town-clerk thereof, to take the oath above-mentioned." Thus the law remained throughout the rest of the provincial period.

§ 49. *The Duties of Assessors.*

The duties of the assessors—once they have been elected and have qualified—may be considered with reference to (1) the time of assessment, (2) the nature of the list, and (3) the time of return and to whom returnable. *First*, as to the time of making the assessment. The plan of the first few tax acts under the provincial charter, of fixing a date, usually a month or two ahead, not later than which the assessment must be completed, was discarded in 1694, was revived in 1695 and was finally abandoned in 1696, as the accompanying requirement that the completed tax list be delivered to the treasurer by a certain date was found sufficient. *Second*, as to the nature of the tax lists, we find an uninterrupted improvement. The act of June 24th, 1692–'3, is silent on this point. The supplementary act of December 15th, 1692–'3,[1] requires particulars "both of polls and estate within such town, with an addition of all polls and estate which were before omitted, as well noting the names of all persons whom through age and infirmity they expect should be exempted from the poll tax as others." Beginning with the act of June 18th–20th, 1694–'5,[2] we find the requirement of "the names of each collector or constable in the said town or precinct, and the respective sums to them committed to gather:" with the act of March 15th, 1694–'5,[3] the requirement of "distinct and perfect lists, therein setting down every partic-

[1] 1692–'3, c. 1.

[2] 1694–'5, c. 2.

[3] 1694–'5, c. 7.

ular person's name and sum, with a notification thereon of the name of the several constables or collectors for each town or precinct, and the sum which each of them are severally to collect:" and with the act of October 29th, 1697,[1] the requirement of a list in three distinct columns, setting forth "what each particular person is to pay * * * against his or her name respectively; the first column to contain the number of polls for which such person is assessed[2] and the sum set upon each of them, the second column to contain the housing, land or other real estate for which such person is assessed and the sum set thereupon, and the third column to contain the sum set by them upon such person for his or her personal estate and faculty;" and of a certificate of the name or names of the collector, constable or constables of each town, together with the sum total of the list to each of them committed—such certificate to be delivered to the treasurer. In all cases the lists and certificates were to be certified by a majority of the commissioners or assessors. Since the date last mentioned, with the exception of the enumeration of the separate parcels of "housing, land, or other real estate" of each taxpayer, which has been dropped, the requirements of the tax lists have remained practically unchanged. The extension by the act of June 11th–July 4th, 1707,[3] of the duties of the assessors in each town so as to include the assessment of "such town's proportion, also to the county and town charges," "under oath to the discharge of that trust according to the rules and directions in the law in that respect," and "under the like penalty for not accepting and serving as is by law directed for the province tax" would seem to indicate that the machinery for the province taxation was at last working efficiently.[4]

[1] 1697, c. 23.

[2] Referring to the number of his slaves or indentured dependents.

[3] 1707, c. 2.

[4] Slow as the development of a satisfactory tax system was in Massachusetts, their first general tax law, 1699–1700, c. 26, was passed fourteen years before New York's first one, June 14th, 1713.—Schwab, History of New York Property Tax, 56.

§ 50. *The Completion of the Assessment.*

Thirdly, The complicated act of assessment was not completed, at least during the first few years of the provincial period, till the town commissioners had met at the shire towns of their respective counties upon a day fixed by the act under which they were making the assessments, had there perfected their respective lists by a common examination and correction of them, and had finally transmitted them, so perfected, by one of their number chosen for the purpose, to the treasurer of the province. At a later period, if there were no commissioners for the towns, the assessors, whether selectmen or trustees acting as such or a separately elected board, were required to deliver not later than a date invariably specified in the tax acts their certified lists to the treasurer. After the final disappearance of the town commissioner from the tax system, the selectmen, trustees or assessors, as the case might be, were required by the act of June 17th, 1796,[1] to deliver at a date not later than that specified by each act to the collector, constable or constables of their respective towns the perfected tax lists, and to the provincial treasurer their certificates of collectors' or constables' names, and the gross sum apportioned to each to collect.

§ 51. *Difficulties of Assessment.*

If evidence were lacking of the difficulty experienced by the new provincial government in obtaining satisfactory assessors, such evidence would be supplied in abundance by the different provisions of the drastic tax act of June 18th–20th, 1694–'95.[2] Beside the measures already mentioned, this act provides that "if any person be chosen to said place [of assessor] and refuse to attend such service (which he shall forthwith declare whether he accept or no), he shall pay as a fine five pounds if in Boston, Charlestown, Salem, Ipswich, or

[1] 1796, c. 3.

[2] 1694–'5, c. 2.

Newbury, and in any other town forty shillings." A penalty for the neglect by assessors to do the work after taking the oath, unaccountably omitted by the framers of the above act, was introduced into the next one,[1] the following September, in the shape of a forfeiture of the whole sum apportioned to the offending assessor's town, though the penalty for declining to take the oath now drops out. The next tax act[2] adds the alternative of imprisonment, in case no property of the assessors can be found to be levied upon in satisfaction of the execution. All these penalties are then forgotten for a couple of years, then revived together in two successive acts,[3] again omitted,[4] then applied again with increased vigor for three more acts,[5] until, in the general act of March 20th, 1699–1700,[6] and in its successive re-enactments,[7] and in the general act of October 3d–7th, 1730,[8] the penalty of forfeiture for refusing to take the assessor's oath, of five pounds for Boston and forty shillings for other towns, and of proportional sums for failing "duly to attend and observe all such warrants as during the time of their office they shall receive from the treasurer and receiver-general of this province, pursuant to any act or acts to be made and passed by the great and general court or assembly of the same, for the assessing and apportioning any province rate or tax upon the inhabitants or estates within the towns whereof they are assessors," became an established feature of the provincial tax system.

[1] 1694–'5, c. 12.

[2] 1694–'5, c. 19.

[3] 1696, c. 16 and 1697, c. 6.

[4] 1697, c. 23.

[5] 1698, c. 15, 1698, c. 24 and 1699–1700, c. 14.

[6] 1699–1700, c. 26.

[7] 1703–'4, c. 3; 1706–'7, c. 3; 1709, c. 1; 1716–'7, c. 4; 1717–'8, c. 5; 1722–'3, c. 4.

[8] 1730, c. 1.

§ 52. *Compensation to Assessors.*

It did not occur to the bustling reformers who framed the act of June 18th–20th, 1694–5,[1] that the tax laborer is worthy of his hire. Perhaps it was because the province had not yet emerged from that stage of politico-social development in which the attempt to tax every one according to his faculty "is seen in the enforced participation in the administration,"[2] that, until the act of June 17th, 1696,[3] the assessors received no pecuniary compensation for the performance of their really difficult and thankless task. Beginning with that act, each assessor was allowed two shllings per day "for each day he attended the service;" and with the addition of the adverb "necessarily" before the participle "spent," and of the adjective "whole" before the noun "day," to cut off any chance of the assessors' amassing fortunes at the public expense, the clause allowing them this munificent remuneration was retained until 1730,[4] when the compensation was doubled.

§ 53. *Collectors: Choice, Number, etc.*

The collection of taxes, though by no means without its difficulties, has been the source of but little trouble compared with that experienced in obtaining just and adequate assessments; and the changes in the plan of procedure in it have been comparatively few and slight. As has already been seen, it is that very ancient and respectable town officer, the constable, who from the earliest times in the Massachusetts colony numbered among his duties the collection of taxes; and the first tax act under the provincial charter[5] avails itself of his services for this work as a matter of course. The sup-

[1] 1694–'5, c. 2.

[2] Seligman, The General Property Tax, *Political Science Quarterly*, V., 38.

[3] 1696, c. 3.

[4] 1730, c. 1.

[5] 1692–'3, c. 4.

plementary act of December 15th, 1692–3,[1] among its provisions for improving the tax system, enables the selectmen or assessors in each town, if they see fit, to appoint a collector or collectors. The preference of the people for the separate officer is sufficiently evident; for, though the provision referred to did not extend beyond the tax then authorized, and was repeated but once (June 18th–20th, 1694–'5[2]), and then only temporarily, till the general tax act of March 20th, 1699–1700,[3] gave that officer a permanent place in the system, yet there is no one of the thirteen tax acts passed during the period mentioned that does not incidentally recognize the collector as an officer on an equal footing with the constable.

The acts of December 15th, 1692–'3,[1] and June 18th–20th, 1694–'5,[2] provided that the election of collectors for the taxes then voted should be by the selectmen and the assessors of the towns where they were chosen; but the general act of March 20th, 1699–1700,[4] provided that the choice of collectors should be made by the voters, at the same time that they chose assessors and other town officers, viz., at the annual town meeting in March. This still remains the rule. The number of collectors to be chosen was not fixed in any act. The act of October 3rd–7th, 1730,[5] empowered constables and collectors, though superseded by others appointed in their stead, to go ahead and complete the collection of such taxes as they were responsible for.

§ 54. *General Development.*

It has been shown how, in the history of assessments, the government, in order to frustrate frequent attempts on the part of individual citizens and even of whole towns to avoid the

[1] 1692–'3, c. 41.

[2] 1694–'5, c. 2.

[3] 1699–1700, c. 26.

[4] 1699–1700, c. 26.

[5] 1730, c. 1.

payment of taxes, were obliged to follow up the delinquents step by step, minutely prescribing the duties of every officer concerned in the assessment as well as of the taxpayers themselves, and affixing severe penalties for neglect or malfeasance in the case of any one of them, until finally in cases where injunctions and penalties proved alike unavailing the court of general sessions for the county was called in to appoint assessors and force an assessment. It is interesting to note a development almost precisely similar, although one naturally later in manifesting itself, in the case of collections. The development of the provincial tax system was nearly completed during the first decade of the second charter; but like the vulnerable spot in the heel of Achilles, there was still one fatal defect in its machinery for assessing and collecting taxes from people who did not want to pay them; though it was not till after the lapse of half a century that this defect appears to have been discovered, or at least to have been taken advantage of to any disturbing degree. The act of February 8th, 1745–6,[1] recites that "whereas no provision is made in the Act entitled an Act directing how rates and taxes granted by the general assembly, as also county, town and precinct rates, shall be assessed and collected," for appointing collectors or constables where towns neglect to choose them, "whereby, unless there be some remedy, the good design of said Act, to secure the payment of the taxes granted by the general assembly, will be frustrated," the general court now enact that in such cases the sheriff, a county officer, shall collect the rates. In the cases of both assessments and collections, then, it was found necessary to have final recourse to permanent county officers for the efficient carrying out of legislative measures for the taxation of the smaller political units.

§ 55. *Qualifications of Collectors.*

No qualifications are specified as being required of con-

[1] 1745–'6, c. 19.

stables. The general act of November 25th–December 9th, 1692–3,[1] "for the establishment of forms of oaths," prescribes the following form for constables:

"Whereas you, A B, are chosen constable within the town of C for one year now following, and until other be chosen and sworn in your place, you do swear, that you will carefully intend the preservation of the peace, the discovery and preventing all attempts against the same, that you will duly execute all warrants which shall be sent unto you from lawful authority, and faithfully attend all such directions in the laws and orders of court as are or shall be committed to your care, that you will faithfully and with what speed you can collect and levy all such fines, distresses, rates, assessments and sums of money for which you shall have sufficient warrants according to law, rendering an account thereof, and paying in the same according to the direction in your warrant. And with like faithfulness, speed and diligence will serve all writs, executions and distresses in private causes betwixt party and party, and make returns thereof duly into the same court where they are returnable. And in all these things you shall deal seriously and faithfully whilst you shall be in office, without any sinister respects of favor or displeasure. So help you God."

The acts above referred to as authorizing the election of separate collectors in those two cases mention only the conventional requirements of "ability" and "sufficiency"; while the general act of March 20th, 1699–1700,[2] authorizes the choice of "one or more meet person or persons." Though there is no form of oath prescribed for collectors, nor any reference to such an oath, with the exception of the form prescribed in the general act of November 29th–December 19th, 1720–1,[3] which applied only to collectors of local rates, yet the omission of such a requirement was not in accordance with the usual practice of the provincial government.

[1] 1692–'3, c. 35.

[2] 1699–1700, c. 26.

[3] 1720–'1, c. 7.

§ 56. *Duties of Collectors.*

The duty of the collector or of the constable acting as such was twofold; first, to collect from each taxpayer on his list the sum which such taxpayer had been assessed; and, secondly, to pay over all moneys by him so collected to the provincial treasurer. For aiding the collector in the performance of the first of these duties the act of June 24th, 1692--3,[1] gave him, in the case of persons refusing or neglecting to make payment of the sums so assessed upon them, the power of levying the same by distress and sale of goods of such persons, returning any overplus; and the severer act of December 15th–16th, 1692-3,[2] added the further penalty, in cases where no goods appeared to levy upon, of the commitment of such person by the collector, under warrant from two or more of the assessors, to the common jail, there to be kept without bail or mainprize until payment be made. These severe provisions, thus early adopted, were retained throughout the provincial period with no change except that the power of instituting proceedings against delinquent taxpayers seems by the act of March 7th, 1695–6,[3] to have been vested for a time in the provincial treasurer. By a subsequent act[4] the previous plan was restored.

A date was always fixed, usually from three to ten months ahead, not later than which the constables and collectors were required to make their payments to the provincial treasurer; with which act their labors and the history of the particular tax was completed. For failure to comply with this requirement, the act of June 24th, 1693–4,[5] imposed a penalty of the payment by the offending collector of ten pounds in money, and all arrears of the assessments committed to him; the act of

[1] 1992–'3, c. 4.

[2] 1692–'3, c. 41.

[3] 1695–'6, c. 17, § 4.

[4] 1743–'4, c. 11.

[5] 1693–'4, c. 4.

December 15th, 1692–3[1] enabled the treasurer "to levy all such sum or sums of money by distress and sale of such defective constable or collector's goods and chattels, returning the overplus (if any there be), and for want of such distress to commit the offender to the common gaol of the county;" and, beginning with the act of June 18th–20th, 1694–5,[2] the following acts add the phrase, "there to remain until the full payment be made." The further security of making every town responsible for any defect in the returns of its constables, which was included in the acts of December 15th, 1692–3,[1] and June 18th–20th, 1694–5,[2] was, for some reason, perhaps through oversight, not again repeated until the general act of March 20th, 1699–1700.[3]

At first the treasurer sent his warrants for assessments and collections directly to the assessors and collectors in the different towns; but beginning in 1696, he was required to send them under cover to the sheriff or marshal of each county, who should distribute them forthwith to the assessors and collectors.

§ 57. *Exclusive Taxes.*

The mind of the provincial legislator was not always clear as to the real difference between an assessed tax and an excise. The early history of the province of Massachusetts furnishes us with a curious example of this confusion in a group of tax laws,[4] nominally, "for granting unto his majesty an excise upon wines, liquors, and other strong drink sold by retail;" but in reality laying an exclusive income tax—the only attempt at laying an exclusive tax before 1749–'50, when the act of April 20th provided for an exclusive tax upon calashes,

[1] 1692–'3, c. 41.

[2] 1694–'5, c. 2.

[3] 1699–1700, c. 26.

[4] 1710–'11, c. 11; 1711–'12, c. 3; 1712–'13, c. 2; 1713–'14, c. 2; 1714, c. 2; 1715–'16, c. 9.

chairs, chaises, chariots and coaches. But this act was, for reasons touching other features of it, disallowed by the English privy council.

It is of the essential nature of those taxes commonly called "indirect," including excises, that, being computed at a fixed per cent. of a variable base, the amount of the tax can be only approximately estimated in advance; while in the case of a "direct" tax, either a fixed percentage of a variable base may be required of the taxpayer, in which case the amount of the tax can be only approximately estimated as before; or an ascertained sum may be demanded of him, irrespective of the ratio which that sum bears to the money value of the property taxed. In each of the six acts above referred to, the general court not only determined the whole sum to be raised by the tax, but apportioned that sum among the counties of the province; delegating to the justices of the respective courts of general sessions of the peace, the power to "levy, lay and duly apportion" the "excise" "according to their good discretion to and upon the several taverners, wineholders, common victualers and retailers within their county." But if these assessments as made were not excises neither were they license fees, even though as in each of these acts the renewing of an old license or the granting of a new one was made contingent upon the assessments being paid, for the amounts of fees are fixed being the same for all persons for the same services rendered or the same privileges granted. In the case of these acts, this was rendered impossible in practice by the apportionment among the counties.

CHAPTER II.

INDIRECT TAXATION.

§ 58. *The Organization of Imposts.*

The organization of the force for administering indirect taxes in Massachusetts has always been more simple than that of the force for administering direct taxes. The two great departments of indirect taxes in Massachusetts, in the order of their financial importance, have been the imposts (with which may be included tonnage of shipping) and the excises; and in that order we shall take up their history.

The error of the first impost act under the provincial charter[1] of introducing into the customs administration a division of responsibility, in providing for the appointment of more than one "commissioner," was corrected two years later in an act[2] providing "that there be one fit person and no more * * appointed * * as a commissioner and collector, to have the general inspection, care and management of the said office of impost." From that time until, by the adoption of the federal constitution in 1789, all customs were relinquished by the states to the federal government, the head of the customs administration in Massachusetts was a single officer, though his title was changed by the act of December 9th–10th, 1698,[3] to that of "commissioner and receiver." The first act abovementioned[1] provided for the employment, in addition to the commissioners, of "so many officers under them as they shall find needful." By the act of June 8th–20th, 1694–5,[2] provision

[1] 1692–'3, c. 5.
[2] 1694–'5, c. 1.
[3] 1698, c. 17.

was made for the employment of "so many officers under him as the said commissioner, with the advice of the treasurer for the time being, * * shall think necessary for the well ordering and managing of the affairs relating to said office, and the better to prevent frauds;" by that of December 9th–10th, 1698,[1] the number of "deputy receivers," as the subordinate officers were now called, was limited to one for each port beside that in which the commissioner resided; by that of March 27th–29th, 1702–3,[2] the number of officers was again enlarged to "so many * * as the commissioner shall think needful to assist therein;" while the ultimate form of the subordinate organization of the department was attained when, by the act of December 20th, 1739,[3] "a deputy receiver in each port and other places," was authorized.

§ 59. *Commissioners: Appointment; Qualifications.*

In the method of the appointment and commissioning of the customs officers, there was but one change under the second charter. The first customs act[4] vested the nomination, appointment and commissioning of the commissioners of impost in the governor and council, and the same act that reduced the number of commissioners to one[5] vested the nomination and appointment of that officer in the general court, while his commission only was to issue from the governor. From the beginning each commissioner selected his own subordinates, although when the number of commissioners was reduced to one[5] the advice of the provincial treasurer was at least nominally essential to the choice, a limitation which was abandoned in 1698.[6]

No act prescribed qualification for either commissioners or subordinates, the question of fitness being left entirely to the

[1] 1698, c. 16.
[2] 1702–'3, c. 1.
[3] 1739–'40, c. 13.
[4] 1692–'3, c. 5.
[5] 1694–'5, c. 1.
[6] The last act in which it was required was 1698, c. 16.

judgment of the appointing authority. The initial customs act of the second charter[1] required that the commissioners and all officers employed by them be sworn "to deal truly and faithfully" in the execution of their duties; the reformatory act of June 8th–20th, 1694–5,[2] declared that "the commissioners and all other under officers, before their entering upon the execution of their respective offices, shall take the oaths appointed to be taking instead of the oaths of supremacy and allegiance, and repeat and subscribe the declaration,[3] * * as also shall be sworn to deal truiely and faithfully in the execution of their respective offices;" but with the act of June 18th–19th, 1697, the simple oath "to deal truly and faithfully therein" was restored to a permanent place in the impost laws.

§ 60. *Duties of Commissioners.*

The only duty specified in the act of June 24th–28th, 1692–3[1] as devolving upon the commissioners was that "to account with the treasurer for all their collections;" the reformatory act of June 8th–20th, 1694–5,[2] required the commissioner "to keep fair books of all entries and duties arising by virtue of this act, which books shall be open at all seasonable times to the view and perusal of the treasurer. And the said commissioner shall also account with the treasurer, upon oath, for all monies and payments at the end of every three months; the said oath to be administered before the governor and council, and pay in all such monies as shall be in his hands as the treasurer shall demand it." The important act of June 18th–19th, 1697,[4] omitted the spectacular episode of the second oath before the governor and council, required an accounting as often as the treasurer should demand it and re-

[1] 1692–'3, c. 5.

[2] 1694–'5, c. 1.

[3] The reference is to certain oaths and a declaration provided for in an act of parliament of I. William and Mary, entitled "An Act for Abrogating the Oaths of Allegiance and Supremacy and appointing other oaths," and mentioned in the provincial charter of Massachusetts.

[4] 1697, c. 3.

quired the commissioner to administer an oath to persons suspected of making short entries. Four years later the business of the customs had increased to such a degree that the commissioner was required to "attend in the office from nine to twelve of the clock in the forenoon, and from two to five of the clock in the afternoon"[1] —a practice thereafter substantially continued. It was not till seventeen years later that the statement of the duties of the commissioner took the form which it afterward retained, by the additional requirement that the commissioner keep "a particular accompt of every vessel, so that the dutys, impost and tunnage arising on the said vessel may appear,"[2] and that he exhibit his books not only to the treasurer and receiver-general, but to "any other person or persons whom this court shall appoint."

The first intimation of a definition of the duties of subordinate customs officers is contained in that clause of the act of June 8th–20th, 1694–5,[3] which grants to the single commissioner, then first provided for, the power "to grant them warrants" for assisting in "the well ordering and managing the affairs relating to said office and the better to prevent frauds." An administrative advance was made when the act of December 9th–10th, 1698,[4] directed the commissioner "to grant warrants to such deputy-receivers for their said place, and to collect and receive the imposts for all wines, liquors, goods and merchandizes that shall be imported into such port, and to render the accompts thereof, and pay in the same to the said commissioner and receiver."

No penalties for non-feasance or mal-feasance were provided for either commissioners or subordinates.

§ 61. *Powers of Commissioners.*

It is in the powers vested in the customs officers in the pro-

[1] 1701–'2, c. 16.
[2] 1718–'19, c. 12.
[3] 1694–'5, c. 1.
[4] 1698, c. 17.

secution of their duties that the greatest number of important changes was made. It would be difficult to find a better example of what elsewhere in this essay has been called automatic legislation, by which is meant legislation requiring certain things to be done and providing no means for enforcing the requirement, than the act of June 24th–28th, 1692–3.[1] By this first customs act of the second charter no special power whatever was given to the commissioners themselves looking toward the enforcement of the provisions of the act; and the power vested by the act in "such as are impowred or improved by the commissioners," or in "the informer or discoverer," "to search, according to law, all manner of houses, cellars and warehouses," for goods believed to have been smuggled, was hedged about by the requirement that such search should "be made in the day-time, and within the space of one month after the offense supposed to have been committed," "with one constable or more," and "by warrant from the lieutenant-governor or any two justices of the peace within this province (to that purpose first obtained)."

§ 62. *Their Powers Increased.*

The first section of "An Act for the Better Collecting the Impost and Excise, and Preventing Frauds,"[2] provided "that such officer or officers as are or shall be impowered and appointed by the commissioners for impost and excise, shall have power and are hereby authorized to enter on board any ship or vessel, there to make search, or to attend the unloading of any such ship or vessel, the better to prevent fraud, and to secure the true payment of the duties, so by act or acts for or relating to the impost and excise is imposed." By the act of June 11th–22d, 1695–6,[3] the commissioner was empowered to "sue for and recover, in any of his majestie's court of record, or before any justice of the peace, where the matter is not

[1] 1692–'3, c. 5.

[2] 1693, c. 5.

[3] 1695–'6, c. 1.

above his cognizeance, any sum or sums of money that are or shall grow due according to agreement made for any of the aforesaid duties, where the party or parties with whom such agreement is or may be made, shall neglect or refuse to pay the same." The strongly reactionary law of December 9th–10th, 1698,[1] brought about by the large decrease in the income from customs since the passage of the impost act of the previous June,[2] substituted in place of all the above the simple power of the commissioner "to sue the master of any ship or vessel for the impost or duty for so much of the lading of wines, liquors, goods, wares, and merchandizes imported therein according to the manifest by him to be given upon oath as aforesaid, or shall remain not entered, and the duty or impost thereof not paid;" and even this provision was dropped after the next act.[3] The preamble of the act of March 27th–29th, 1703,[4] is significant of the inefficiency of the customs administration under the then existing law. Yet the act was superseded in three months, and neither the section conferring upon the commissioners "the same power in the searching for, seizing, securing and prosecuting for goods imported and not duely entered as are by law granted to the commissioners of excise," nor that authorizing them to "procure boats or vessels, and when need shall be, hire men to go in them," was afterward repeated. The unusual development which, after building up for the customs officers such ample powers, left them at the end of eleven years in nearly the same condition in which they were at the beginning, is due to the fact that for the first five years, the period during which the powers of the

[1] 1698, c. 17.

[2] 1698, c. 16.

[3] 1700–'1, c. 7.

[4] 1702–'3, c. 1. "For the more effectual securing of the payment of the several duties of impost, tunnage of shipping, and excise, arising within this province, according to the rates set in and by the acts and laws now in force for granting and continuing of the same, for the avoiding of disputes, and for direction to the collectors and receivers of the said duties."

customs officers were enlarged the most, the commissioners of impost were also commissioners of excise—a department of the public service in which larger administrative powers have generally been found necessary;—and it is likewise due to the fact that, after the organization of a separate excise department in 1697, the duties of the customs officers were correspondingly lighter. As a matter of fact, the phraseology of former laws, conferring identical powers upon the commissioners of both departments, was left unaltered, through sheer inertia, for several years after their separation took place.

§ 63. *Commodities Taxed.*

The policy of provincial Massachusetts in the selection of commodities for indirect taxation, both imposts and excises, was simple, uniform and correct. Broadly stated, it was to exempt altogether the necessities of life and to tax the conveniences only lightly, leaving the burden of the indirect taxation to be borne by the luxuries; and among luxuries choosing for the heaviest duties those the use of which was oftenest carried to harmful excess. From the first customs act of the second charter,[1] salt, cotton-wool, provisions and all commodities produced in New England were specifically exempted from all duties. Not only were the commodities produced in New England almost exclusively necessities, but the formation of a sort of customs union between the New England colonies was quite in accord with the growing idea of a solidarity of interests between them, which, from the first, Massachusetts had been foremost in recognizing.

That the act of September 8th, 1721–2,[2] which levied heavy specific and *ad valorem* duties upon certain commodities imported into Massachusetts from New Hampshire and upon others exported from Massachusetts into New Hampshire, was no voluntary departure from this policy, is evident from a con-

[1] 1692–'3, c. 5.
[2] 1721–'2, c. 5.

sideration of the facts in the case as recited in the preamble to the act in question.[1] The selection for these duties, intended to be prohibitive, of luxuries coming from New Hampshire and necessities going to it, was consistent with the avowed purpose of the act to retaliate severely upon the offending government and in the end brake up its exclusiveness.

§ 64. *English Goods.*

There was, however, one country the productions of which Massachusetts, with shrewd judgment, wished to utilize as the source of a considerable and certain revenue without injuring the trade. From the initiatory customs act of the province[2] all goods not specifically taxed or exempted were subjected to a small *ad valorem* import duty. By the act of June 18th–19th, 1697,[3] a discrimination was made against English goods by imposing upon them a duty more than twice that to which other non-enumerated goods were subjected. And although this rate was reduced one-half for the next three years, the higher rate was then restored, to be maintained uniformly until 1719. A prolonged and bitter controversy took place between the two branches of the general court in that year upon the question of disregarding the king's recent instructions to the governor to withhold his consent from all bills imposing duties upon English goods. The representatives contended pertinaciously and acrimoniously not only for the continuance of a revenue which, in their judgment, the province could not then relinquish without serious inconvenience, but (being

[1] "Whereas, the government of New Hampshire do exact and take two shillings a thousand for every thousand of boards brought down the river commonly called Piscataqua River and transported into this province (though the trees out of which the boards are made grow upon lands within this province, and are cut at mills in the county of York), altho' the inhabitants of this government have equal right with the inhabitants of the province of New Hampshire, to pass up and down the aforesaid river, by grant and purchase; which exaction is therefore altogether unjust and oppressive."

[2] 1692–'3, c. 5.

[3] 1697, c. 3.

pleased to regard their relation to the general court as identical with that of the house of commons to the English parliament) especially for what they consistently if not logically contended was their sole prerogative—the originating of all financial legislation for the province.[1] The council, on their part, justified their resistance by protesting their regard for the best interests of the province in their solicitude to secure the passage of the impost bill in such a form that the governor could consent to it, and the king would not disallow it. Not until it became evident that for once the council were more determined than themselves, did the representatives surrender. From the date of this surrender, though it was understood at the time to be only a waiver of the question for the current year, English goods, and from 1739,[2] British goods were admitted into Massachusetts free of duty.

§ 65. *Tariff Classification.*

As regards the classification of articles, the early provincial tariffs were much more elaborate than later ones. The most marked example of this tendency to simplification is that of the important commodity wine, which from a division into no fewer than nine classes by the first half dozen acts, gradually passed, from time to time, during more than sixty years, through every smaller number, till, in the last fifteen acts, "every sort of wine" paid the same duty. The administrative gain from this simplification must have been considerable.

The experiment made in the act of November 21st, 1702,[3] of selecting from the residue of unenumerated articles "all wrought silks, except black; gold and silver lace, fringe, thread, twist, and buttons; lace made of silk and thread; silk, gimp, hair and thread fringes; all ribbons and necklaces; all

[1] For the history of this controversy in detail, see the copious extracts from the council records in Acts and Resolves of the Province of Massachusetts Bay, II., 158–161.

[2] 1739–'40, c. 13.

[3] 1702, c. 7.

cast iron, except military stores, and all shoes, pattoons, gloves and perriwiggs," for the imposition of an enormously increased duty was not repeated, as it was found that by this and the other increases of the duty made by the act trade was discouraged to such a degree that the revenue fell off; while the imposition, by the general act of December 5th, 1705–6,[1] of a heavy specific duty upon negroes was for the avowed purpose of discouraging their importation.

The constant staples during the whole provincial period, upon which specific duties were laid, were wine, rum, (and for most of the time other distilled spirits), sugar, molasses and tobacco, and, until 1753, logwood. Tea imported from other English plantations in America was added to the list from 1756; and for a single year, 1764–5,[2] a specific duty was laid upon bar-iron.

§66. *Export Duties; Retaliation.*

The only export duties to be found in the history of Massachusetts are those imposed by the law of September 8th, 1721,[3] entitled "An Act for laying sundry duties on such goods as shall be imported into this Province from the Province of New Hampshire, and on such as shall be exported from this Province thither." The retaliatory nature of this law, already explained in connection with the subject of imposts,[4] was emphasized by the selection of luxuries, such as wines and spirits, for import duties, and of necessities, such as grain and provisions, for export duties. The rates were intended to be prohibitory. A specific duty of ten shillings was laid upon every barrel of beef or pork, five shillings upon every hundred weight of bread, one shilling upon every bushel of wheat, and sixpence upon every bushel of Indian corn or meal, and an *ad valorem* duty of ten per cent. upon "all other sorts of

[1] 1705–'6, c. 10.
[2] 1764–'5, c. 33.
[3] 1721–'2, c. 5.
[4] *Ante*, § 63.

goods, wares and merchandize." The penalty pronounced upon any master of a vessel who should take on board any goods to be transported to New Hampshire before reporting to the impost officers the quantity and value thereof and paying the duties therefor, was the payment of one hundred pounds sterling, "to be recovered by bill, plaint or information, in any of his Majesty's courts of record; the one half of the said forfeiture to be applied for and towards the support of this his Majesty's government, the other half to be to and for the use of him or them that shall inform and sue for the same." The temper of the general court when it passed the law may be inferred from the fact that contrary to its custom in cases where the wisdom of the course was far less problematical than it was here, it set no limit of time to the operation of the act. No record of the repeal of the act is to be found, but it doubtless became a dead letter long before the adoption of the federal constitution in Massachusetts put an end to all state legislation upon interstate commerce.

§ 67. *The Organization of Excises.*

Much more difficulty was experienced in obtaining satisfactory officers for the excise than for the impost, and many more changes were made in the organization of the excise department than in that of the customs; in fact, the trouble with the excise officers was less only than that with the assessors; and it was not so quickly overcome in permanent legislation as that was.

Until 1697 there was but one organization for both departments, the title of the chief officers, while there were more than one, being "commissioners of impost and excise," and, after the reorganization under a single head, "commissioner of impost, excise and tonnage of shipping." The act of June 18th–19th, 1697,[1] provided for a separate organization of the excise department by the appointment of "three fit persons,

[1] 1697, c. 3.

and no more, * * as commissioners and collectors, to have the general inspection, care and management of the said excise office, and whatsoever relates unto the same." The next excise act [1] reduced the number of commissioners to two, while that of June 29th, 1700–1,[2] provided for one commissioner in each county. The next excise act, that of June 18th, 1701–2,[3] presents curious evidence of contemporary dissatisfaction with the work of the excise officers, and of the confusion sometimes existing in the colonial and provincial legislation. By this remarkable act "the justices of the court of general sessions of the peace in each respective county or place within this province * * shall be and are hereby impowered to renew and grant licenses;" "the treasurer of the province shall be the receiver of the said excise, unto whom the respective retailers shall pay in the sum apportioned unto them;" and "the commissioners appointed for collecting and receiving the said excise in the several countys be and hereby are impowered to compound with such retailers for their excise."

§ 68. *A Change of Policy.*

Although the inconsistency of the clause in the last-named act, referring to the treasurer, with that referring to the commissioners is evident, and, as a matter of fact, no provision had been made by law for the appointment of commissioners for that year, yet the revival of all the provisions of the act in June, 1702,[4] and the reference in the act of November 21st, 1702,[5] to "the commissioners and receivers that are or shall be named and appointed by this court," while the clause appointing the treasurer to be receiver is omitted, renders it probable that the plan of a commissioner for each county was

[1] 1698, c. 16.
[2] 1700–'1, c. 8.
[3] 1701–'2, c. 15.
[4] 1702, c. 1.
[5] 1702, c. 7.

not discontinued through these years. However this may have been, it is certain that the commissioner disappeared with the act of July 31st, 1703–4.[1] This act, annually renewed for the next six years,[2] was, in its method of vesting the powers to grant licenses and collect the excise, itself a revival of the system which we may presume to have been intended by the act of June 18th, 1701–2,[3] and the characteristic feature of which was its resort to the services of a branch of the regular judiciary in the effort to fasten upon each person affected by the excise law the full sum which he ought in justice to pay. That the system was regarded as extraordinary and temporary is evidenced, not so much by the fact that it was enacted for only a year at a time—the practice of the provincial assembly in most of its early legislation—as by many incidental references in the acts themselves, such as that the acts "will be necessary to remain and abide still in force in this time of war," and "are necessary to be revised and further continued until other and better provision be made."[4]

§ 69. *The Pseudo-excises of 1710–16.*

Concerning the so-called excises from 1710–11 to 1715–16 inclusive we have already spoken under the head of direct taxation, to which class of taxes they properly belong, from the fact of their having been apportioned in fixed sums among the counties, by the general court, and among the individuals taxed, according to the judgment of the justices. During these years the province, by its anxiety in a time of war to realize a sufficient and certain income from the excise, found itself in a position where there was no excise at all, properly speaking, the place of that indirect tax having been taken by a special direct tax upon a single class of inhabitants. Having

[1] 1703–'4, c. 5.

[2] 1704–'5, c. 6; 1705–'6, c. 2; 1706–'7, c. 1; 1707–'8, c. 1; 1708–'9, c. 1, and 1709–'10, c. 1.

[3] 1701–'2, c. 15.

[4] 1708–'9, c. 1.

passed through the development above outlined, ending in a period of suspended animation, the excise system of provincial Massachusetts attained what may be regarded as its normal form when, by the act of June 27th, 1716–17,[1] the system of 1700–1 was revived with the single modification of providing for more than one commissioner in each county.

§ 70. *Subordinate Excise Officers.*

As in the case of the impost, the number of subordinate excise officers has never been fixed by law, these points having been left to the discretion of the chief officers. The only feature here demanding attention is the practice that prevailed throughout the period during which the excise was administered by the judiciary, of utilizing the services of regular county and town officers—"grand jurours, sheriffs, under-sheriffs, constables, tythingmen"—as well as "such other persons as shall be appointed by the respective courts of general sessions of the peace" for certain duties in connection with the excise.

From the separate organization of the excise department[2] to the present time, the commissioners and collectors of excise have been appointed by the general court and commissioned by the governor; although the act of June 16th–29th, 1721,[3] in harmony with the tendency already pointed out to fall back in an emergency upon the judiciary, provided that commissioners should be appointed "by the general sessions of the peace, where it shall happen that such commissioners refuse to accept said office, or be removed by death, etc.," to which list of contingencies the court, taught by experience, soon[4] added a third, "or mismanagement." Subordinate excise officers, like subordinate customs officers, have been appointed by their superiors, with the exception above noted of the

[1] 1716–'17, c. 1.
[2] 1697, c. 3.
[3] 1721, c. 1.
[4] June 28th–29th, 1726–'7, c. 11.

employment of county and town officers during the judiciary administration.

§ 71. *Qualifications; Oaths.*

Concerning the qualifications and oaths required of the commissioners of excise while they were still commissioners of impost we have already spoken. The same conventional requirement of "fitness" and the same form of oath, "to deal truly and faithfully therein," were continued in the law providing for the separate organization of the excise.[1] It was not until after the period of the judiciary administration, beginning in June, 1701–2, after four years with separate commissioners, and continuing fifteen years, through the Indian war, that, by the act of June 27th, 1716–17,[2] in which the final organization of the excise was formulated, a degree of responsible independence was infused into the administration of it by the requirement that, in addition to an oath "to take care of the due execution of this law, and to prosecute the breakers of it," each commissioner should "give bond to the justices at their first general sessions for the peace in their respective counties, with sufficient security, for the faithful discharge of his duty, and that they [he] will duly pay in the money he shall collect to the treasurer of the province for the time being." Finally, by the act of June 26th–28th, 1727,[3] the amount of the bond required was fixed at "double the sum that is usually received for excise annually in said county."

§ 72. *Duties of Excise Officers.*

Even after the separation of the excise from the impost, no difference whatever was made in the duties of the commissioners of the respective departments, until, in the act of July 31st, 1703–4,[4] the commissioner of excise entirely disappeared by

[1] 1697, c. 3.

[2] 1716–'17, c. 1.

[3] 1727, c. 1.

[4] 1703–'4, c. 5.

the complete shifting of the administration of the excise upon the justices of the county courts. When, at the end of their fifteen years' administration, the history of the excise as a fully independent department begins, the duties properly belonging to a commissioner of excise were better understood in the province; and in the course of the first three acts of the period then inaugurated, they were developed in the form in which they have since remained. By the law of June 27th, 1716–17,[1] each commissioner must "carefully examine the accompts of every licensed person in his respective county, and demand, sue for, and receive the several sums due from them by this act, and the same shall pay into the public treasury of this province;" by that of June 16th–29th, 1721,[2] he must make his payments to the treasurer "within six months from the date of his commission, and so from time to time within that space of six months, as long as he shall continue in such office;" by that of June 28th–29th, 1726–7,[3] they "shall give in an account under their hands of the particular sums they receive, together with the names of the persons of whom received, unto the treasurer, upon oath," and at the time of receiving any money, the said collectors shall give two receipts, of the same tenor and date, mentioning what sum or sums they have received from every taverner, inn-holder, common victualer and retailer; one of which receipts to be by the same taverner, innholder, common victualer or retailer returned to the court of the general sessions of the peace, within the respective counties, at the next session of such court, and the clerks of the said courts shall within twenty days after the receipt thereof, transmit the same to the treasurer or receiver-general."

§ 73. *Powers of Excise Officers.*

The first differentiation of the powers of the commissioners of excise from those of the commissioner of impost appeared

[1] 1716–'17, c. 1.
[2] 1721, c. 1.
[3] 1726–'7, c. 11.

in the act providing for the separation of the two departments,[1] when the commissioners of excise were by implication given the power to farm the excise. After the specific authorization of such a course by the act of June 27th, 1698,[2] the only mention of farming the excise, for thirty-nine years, is a reference to it as a contingency in the act of July 14th–18th, 1699–1700,[3] the first separate excise act under the provincial charter, and in the revival of that act for one year, by the act of June 8th–26th, 1702.[4] It is difficult to understand why the power "to sue for and recover any sum or sums of money due or to be due from any retailer or retailers" should have been given by the act of June 29th, 1700–1,[5] to the commissioners of the preceeding act[6] and not to those of the acts that followed it. It is equally difficult to see why, in the event of any brewer's or distiller's neglecting to make entry of goods or to take the oath, as by law required, the power "to enter into the brewery or still-house of such brewer or distiller, respectively, and the dependencies thereof, or other houses, cellars, vaults or places where they shall be informed any beer, ale, spirits or strong liquors, brewed or distilled as aforesaid, are laid with intent to be concealed in elusion of the law, and to search for, seize and secure, in order to trial and conviction, all such beer, ale, spirits or strong liquors,"[1] should have been bestowed upon the commissioner of excise in an act devolving the proper duties of that officer upon other officers, and this just as the commissioner was about to disappear altogether from the excise system for a period of fifteen years. Upon the reorganization of the excise system in 1716, the powers delegated to the commissioner of excise were those of appointing under-officers

[1] 1697, c. 3.
[2] 1698, c. 16.
[3] 1699-1700, c. 15.
[4] 1702, c. 1.
[5] 1700-'1, c. 8.
[6] 1699-1700, c. 15.
[7] 1702, c. 7.

upon oath, and inspecting the houses of all such as were licensed or suspected of selling without license.

§ 74. *Excise Classification.*

The same cumbersome detail of classification which was noted in the early provincial impost is found in the excise of the same years; but the process of simplification was here applied much earlier and much more thoroughly than there. For example, wines, after having been scheduled in ten or eleven classes for eleven years, were not classified at all after 1716. The radicalness of this change was doubtless largely due to the intervention of the period of the judiciary administration of the excise, during the last six years of which no schedules at all were made by the general court. As in the case of the imposts, wine and spirits formed the basis of the excise throughout the provincial period; malt liquors, metheglin, perry and cider, the only other commodities that figured in the list during the first decade, disappearing altogether when the excise was handed over to the county judges in 1710, except perry and cider for the single year 1716–7.[1] Nor was any other commodity added to the slender list of wines and spirits until, in 1737,[2] at the same time that the rates on these were largely increased, an excise was placed upon limes and lemons, coaches and chariots, chaises with four wheels and other chaises, calashes and chairs. Of these added commodities only lemons and limes survived the expiration of that act, being retained on the list, with the addition of oranges in 1748,[3] till the end of the provincial period; although calashes, chairs, chaises, chariots and coaches, together with tea, coffee, arrack, snuff and chinaware, were placed upon the excise list by an act passed April 20th, 1750,[4] but disallowed two years later by the English privy council.

[1] 1716–'7, c. 1.

[2] 1737–'8, c. 1.

[3] 1748–'9, c. 4.

[4] 1749–'50, c. 21.

CHAPTER III.

THE LOTTERIES.

§ 75. *Private Lotteries in Massachusetts.*

It was during the third quarter of the eighteenth century, at the same time with the land bank hereafter described, and other unsound financial schemes, that the policy of raising public funds by lottery became settled for a time in Massachusetts. To be sure, lotteries were no new thing in the eighteenth century. Not unknown in principle to the ancient Greeks and Romans, and spreading from Italy over continental Europe, in the middle ages, they were introduced into England as early as 1569. During the seventeenth century the passion for this kind of gaming increased to such an extent that in Queen Anne's reign lotteries were denounced as public nuisances. Unfortunately, the act of parliament passed in 1709, prohibiting all private undertakings of this kind, did not apply to the colonies; where, although an assembly of ministers at Boston as early as 1699 denounced them as "cheats," and their managers as "pillagers of the people," lotteries of various forms found a wide and growing patronage. The first legislation in Massachusetts bearing upon the subject was "An Act for the Suppressing of Lotteries," passed November 7th, 1719.[1] The preamble of this act recites that "there have lately been set up within this province certain mischievous and unlawful games, called lotteries, whereby the children and servants of several gentlemen, merchants and traders, and other unwary people, have been drawn into a vain and foolish expence of money, which tends to the utter ruin and impoverishment

[1] 1719–'20, c. 8. Acts and Resolves, II., 149–'50.

of many families, and is to the reproach of this government, and against the common good, trade, welfare and peace of the province; for remedy whereof" it is enacted: 1. That all such lotteries are "public nuisances;" 2. That playing at lotteries is forbidden, and all who set them up or expose them for playing shall be fined two hundred pounds sterling for each offence; 3. That any person convicted of playing at a lottery shall be fined ten pounds sterling for each offence; and 4. That all justices of the peace, sheriffs, under sheriffs, sheriffs' deputies and constables are exhorted to do their utmost to break up the practice.

Fourteen years later it was found necessary to pass a supplementary act.[1] The act of 1719[2] was found insufficient "to put a stop to the practice, but sundry persons have exposed their estates, as well real as personal, to sale by lotteries projected and the tickets disposed of within this province, reserving the drawing of the lots in some of the neighboring colonies or provinces; whereby the good and wholesome design and true intent and meaning of the aforesaid act is very much eluded and evaded, to the great discouragement of trade and industry, and grievous hurt and damage of many unwary people; for remedy whereof" it was enacted: 1. Whoever sets up a lottery shall be fined five hundred pounds. 2. Whoever aids any lottery by printing, writing, or otherwise publishing an account thereof or where tickets may be had, shall be fined one hundred pounds sterling. 3. Whoever sells, exposes for sale, gives or otherwise disposes of lottery tickets shall be fined two hundred pounds sterling. Provided always: 4. "That this act shall not be construed to extend to any lottery allowed by act of parliament or law of this province."

§ 76. *The First Provincial Lottery.*

The proviso at the end of the above-mentioned law is im-

[1] April 26th–30th, 1733. Acts and Resolves, II., 663–'4.
[2] Chap. 8.

portant: it foreshadows a deliberate change in the financial policy of the provincial government. Pronounced and sweeping as is the denunciation of lotteries contained in the foregoing legislation, and severe as are the penalties prescribed for those who should persist in furthering such enterprises, the framers of these laws saw no inconsistency in prohibiting private lotteries as "public nuisances" and setting up a government lottery to increase the public revenues. It was generally believed that few of the evils connected with private lotteries would attach to a lottery established by public authority and conducted under strict regulations. The need for an increase in the public funds was pressing. The king's instruction against the further issues of bills of credit had dried up at last that perennial fountain of public resources. The returns to the managements of lotteries were believed to be both ample and assured, and there were not wanting numerous precedents of government lotteries, both in England and in some of the other colonies. The Virginia Company had realized thirty thousand pounds from a lottery authorized by James I. in 1612, for the benefit of the English colonies, and since 1709, a government lottery had been annually licensed in England, under certain restrictions, by act of parliament. The preamble of the law establishing the first Massachusetts provincial lottery,[1] recites as the reasons for resorting to this method of raising a public revenue, the great expense of the current year, the protection of the sea coast, the defense of the frontier of New England and the protection of the province of Nova Scotia; and the inhabitants already having been subjected to a heavy tax on polls and estates, and a debt still remaining, the representatives wish to raise the debt in the way least burdensome to the inhabitants.

The amount thus intended to be raised was seven thousand five hundred pounds. The plan of this lottery was that of the

[1] 1744-'5, c. 20. Acts and Resolves, II., 195-'9, January 9th- February 4th 1744-'5.

so-called class or Dutch lottery, in which a certain value is divided into a certain number of unequal prizes, and a certain number of lots or "tickets," each lot giving a chance of winning one of the prizes, are sold for a certain sum each, the aggregate price of the tickets being greater than the aggregate value of the prizes; in distinction from the numerical or Genoese lottery, which has more the character of a wager. In this lottery there were twenty-five thousand blank lots and a like number of "benefit" or prize tickets. The details of the plan for selling and drawing the tickets are given in the law establishing the lottery. An important provision was the one permitting subscriptions to be paid, one-fifth in new tenor bills of credit, or in old tenor bills at the rate of four for one, and four-fifths either in like bills or in bills of credit of other colonies not prohibited by law. All tickets remaining unsold at a certain day were to be taken by the directors on account of the province, and any prizes drawn on them were to be covered into the provincial treasury. By a concurrent vote of the general court[1] the directors were forbidden to sell tickets to any Indian, negro, or mulatto, as such a transaction "might prove of mischievous consequence in many respects."

§ 77. *Remonstrances from England.*

The successful drawing of this lottery for sinking the province debt of seven thousand five hundred pounds sterling was followed by the inauguration of a series of no less than fifteen separate enactments, extending over a period of more than eleven years, from 1749 to 1761, either authorizing certain towns and precincts to set up lotteries for making local improvements of a public nature, such as building or repairing bridges, docks and roads, or removing obstructions to navigation, or establishing provincial lotteries for a similar purpose.[2] The lotteries were all to be modeled after that of

[1] February, 1744, Votes and Orders, 219.

[2] 1749–'50, c. 11, to repair Miles bridge in Swanzey; 1750–'1, c. 14, to build a bridge over Parker river, at Oldtown Ferry, Newberry; 1755–'6, c. 3, to build a

1744, and appear to have been successfully managed, so as to raise the small sums, ranging from four hundred to two thousand pounds, needed for these purposes. It could hardly have been expected that the frequency with which lotteries were now resorted to in order to realize such small sums, and for local purposes—no fewer than four local lottery acts were passed in 1759–'60—would escape the notice and unfavorable comment of the lords of trade in London, to whom all provincial legislation affecting trade and commerce was regularly referred by the crown, for their recommendations thereon. In fact, they were not slow in signifying their decided disapproval of this kind of legislation.

"We have had under our consideration," write the lords to Governor Bernard, under the date of April 21st, 1761, "the Laws passed in the Province of Massachusetts, between February and April 1760, amongst which there are several, providing for the temporary and inconsiderable services of Ferrys, Roads &c., by Lotterys, which is a mode of raising money, that in our opinion ought not to be countenanced and hardly to be admitted into practice, upon the most pressing exigency of the State, more especially in the Colonys, where the forms of Government may not admit of those regulations and checks which are necessary to prevent fraud and abuse in a matter so peculiarly liable to them.

"We cannot, therefore, but disapprove these Laws upon their general Principles, but when we consider the unguarded and loose manner in which they are in general framed, the Objections are so many and so strong that We should cer-

bridge over Tetticut river, in Tetticut precinct; 1755–'6, c. 24, to pave Boston neck; 1757–'8, c. 14, to build a bridge over the Saco and Pasumscot rivers; 1758–'9, c. 38, to complete the paving of Boston neck; 1758–'9, c. 39, to repair the highway in Roxbury; 1759–60, c. 10, to repave the causeway on the east side of Sudbury river; 1759–'60, c. 35, to complete the bridge over the Parker river, at Oldtown Ferry; 1759–'60, c. 36, to remove the rocks and shoals in Taunton Great river; 1759–'60, c. 37, to pave Charlestown highway; 1760–'1, c. 15, to complete the repairing of Roxbury highway; 1760–'1, c. 22, to complete the repaving of the causeway on the east side of Sudbury river; 1760–'1, c. 26, to repair Faneuil hall. There was also one to pave Prince street, Boston, the reference to which is not at hand.

tainly have thought it our duty to have laid them before His Majesty for His Majesty's disapprobation were we not restrained by the consideration that the purposes for which they were passed, having been carried into full execution and the Acts had their full operation and effect, some inconvenience might attend the annulling them; but it is our duty to advise that you will not for the future give your Assent to any Laws of the like nature."[1]

Mr. Bollan, too, the well-tried agent of the province in London, though he sought to put the best interpretation possible upon the matter before the board, was too keen an observer not to perceive the seriousness of the situation in the minds of their lordships, and too faithful to the best interests of his principals not to warn them emphatically against their continuance of the lottery policy. "Their lordships then passed to another affair," writes Mr. Bollan to the speaker of the provincial assembly, concerning a meeting of the board at which he was present, "and Lord Sandys having in his hand four acts for lotteries, he inveigh'd against them as mischievous in their nature, destructive to labor and industry, and introductive of the spirit of gaming, ever attended with many ill consequences. In excuse for these acts, I observed that the distresses occasioned by the heavy expence of the war, of which the province had taken so large a part, had probably brought these lotteries into use; and the whole board having concurr'd with his lordship in declaring their evil nature, I told their lordships I wou'd take the first opportunity of acquainting the general Court with their sentiments thereupon. It is needless to say that many of the most able statesmen as well as divines have always declared against the use of lotteries, and being fully persuaded that the continuance of them wou'd prejudice the province's desirable character in the minds of some of their best friends, as well as be disagreeable to others, I think it my duty to recomend a total disuse of them."[2]

[1] Massachusetts Bay, B. T., Vol. 86, p. 44, in Public Record office; quoted in Acts and Resolves, IV., p. 360.

[2] May 8th, 1761, Felt's Massachusetts Archives, Vol. 22, p. 190.

§78. *The Milled-Dollar Lottery.*

Meantime three other lotteries on a much larger scale had been established by law, one for supplying the treasury with twenty-six thousand seven hundred milled dollars,[1] another for raising thirty thousand pounds sterling toward the expense of a military expedition to Canada,[2] and the third for obtaining funds with which to draw in the still outstanding bills of the land bank.[3] None of these lotteries was managed with the success attending that of 1744, upon the plan of which they were all modeled. The reason advanced for establishing the first of them—the need of a speedy supply of the treasury, while the circumstances of the towns had so changed since the last valuation that a just and equal tax could not be laid—appears to have been little more than a pretext. It being found impossible, notwithstanding the mortgaging of a tax of £8,010 for the payment of prizes and the offering of three per cent. interest on prizes unpaid, to dispose of five thousand tickets at the price of three milled dollars per ticket, within two months, as the law required, two supplementary acts[4] twice extended the time of drawing, allowed the payment of subscriptions in province bills and orders on the treasury in place of the coin at first required, raised the interest on unpaid prizes to six per cent. and finally withdrew the requirement as to the number of tickets to be sold before the drawing. It may have been the ill success of this undertaking that moved the representatives to renew their efforts to break up the traffic in private and foreign lottery tickets within the state. "All the good laws made in Massachusetts against lotteries," naïvely complain the fathers, "are rendered ineffectual by the lotteries set up in the neighboring governments, and the sale of tickets in Massachusetts." To the former exemplary fines for publishing in-

[1] 1750-'1, c. 20.
[2] 1757-'8, c. 35.
[3] 1759-'60, c. 2.
[4] 1750-'1, c. 20; 1751-'2, c. 8.

formation in the interest of private lotteries, or disposing of their tickets, were now added another of not more than forty pounds for receiving or purchasing lottery tickets, and the inducement of complete indemnity from punishment for turning state's evidence.

§ 79. *The Canada Expedition Lottery.*

In his speech of March 2nd, 1758,[1] to the general assembly, Governor Pownall urged that provision be made for meeting the expense of defending the frontiers, maintaining the cruiser King George and sending a military expedition to the eastward. It was to comply with the last request, and as a part of those exertions to fit out an expedition against Canada, which Hutchinson says were the greatest in the history[2] of the province, that the act of April 29th, 1758,[3] was passed, providing for the setting up of a lottery to raise thirty thousand pounds. Thomas Hutchinson and James Bowdoin, two of the best financiers in the province and both afterward governors, had already[4] been appointed by the council to act in concert with such other managers as the house might elect. Beside the usual details of the Massachusetts lotteries, it was provided that the prizes should be paid in treasury notes to draw six per cent. interest till the province should be reimbursed by parliament; and a tax of thirty-four thousand pounds, to be collected in 1760, was mortgaged as collateral security. The history of this lottery is soon told. It proved a failure. A minute in the council records under date of October 10th, 1759[5], records a vote of the house that whereas the act passed in the thirty-first year of his present majesty "proved abortive," the managers be directed to pay all moneys by them collected to the province treasurer, and to

[1] Quoted in Acts and Resolves, IV., 142.
[2] History of Massachusetts, Vol. III.
[3] 1757–'8, c. 35, Acts and Resolves, IV., 88–90.
[4] March 20th, 1758, Acts and Resolves, IV., 403.
[5] Council Records, XXIII., 77.

make a full report of the affair; and that the treasurer reimburse all holders of tickets after advertising three weeks in the Boston papers.

§ 80. *The Land Bank Lottery.*

On January 4th, 1760, William Stoddard and others, directors and partners of the late land bank, petitioned the general court for the establishment of a lottery to relieve the distress into which they declared they had been brought by the "unhappy circumstances" attending the management of that scheme, and which had been especially aggravated by the destruction of all their papers in the court-house fire—a calamity which the land-bankers were by no means the only persons who sought to turn to their substantial advantage. The result of this petition was the act of February 13th–14th, 1760[1], "To Raise Money by Lottery for Drawing in Such of the Notes of the Land Bank or Manufactory Scheme as are yet Outstanding." The preamble of this act recites the declarations of the petition:—that there were near one thousand pounds in notes of the land bank still outstanding to be redeemed; that by the death of many of that company, the insolvency of others, and the removal of divers of them out of the province (having alienated their estates in the same), the raising of money by assessment on the rest to pay these bills, now much enhanced by the interest, would greatly burden and distress them; and that the loss of the books, accounts and other papers containing the transactions of that company, by the burning of the court-house in Boston, rendered it difficult or impracticable to proportion an assessment for that purpose justly among the remaining directors and partners.

The purposes of the act are declared to be the paying of the outstanding notes of the company, the putting of "a final end to the perplexed affairs of that company, and the preventing of frequent applications to the court relating thereto,

[1] 1759–'60, c. 2, Acts and Resolves, IV., 288–91.

whereby the public affairs of the province have been greatly interrupted heretofore." The act provides for the establishment, on the usual plan, of one or more lotteries to produce three thousand five hundred pounds sterling for redeeming the land bank notes, together with twelve per cent. of that sum for prizes, any surplus remaining after the bills were drawn in to be covered into the provincial treasury. A memorial of Samuel Stevens,[1] the most indefatigable petitioner of all the land bankers, declaring that, under the severe legislation by which the operations of the company had been put a stop to, he had already redeemed three hundred pounds more than his just proportion of the bills, and praying that he might be reimbursed from the very first money realized from the lottery, was continued from date to date under one pretext or another, a kind of treatment to which the old man had long ago become accustomed. But this lottery prospered little better than the land bank itself had done. Repeated postponements of the date[2] for drawing were without result; and the commissioners appointed long before to wind up the affairs of the bank as expeditiously as possible were again left to take up their weary task of levying assessments upon such of the survivors of that project as were within their reach and collecting what they could.

§ 81. *The Abandonment of the Lottery Policy.*

It may have been to the uncompromising attitude of the lords of trade in their advice to the governor and of Agent Bollan in his recommendation to the speaker of the house towards the lottery policy, to which reference has already been made, that the signal failure of the last-mentioned lottery was due. At any rate, the receipt of the communication referred to was

[1] April 17th, 1761, Council Records, XXIII., 136.

[2] November 25th, 1761, six months; June 12th, 1762–'3, c. 11, to December 1st. There had previously been a postponement to September 28th, by vote of the council and assembly, Council Records, XXIV., 398.

followed by what appeared to be an unqualified abandonment by the province of the lottery policy, not only as a makeshift in the case of the "temporary and inconsiderable services of Ferrys, Roads, etc.," but as a means of providing for the execution of more important projects with which the government with increasing frequency now found itself called upon to deal. It is true that in 1765 an act was passed[1] to establish a lottery, to raise three thousand two hundred pounds sterling for rebuilding a dormitory of Harvard college. But the permission of the lords to Governor Bernard to affix his signature to that bill was obtained only upon the governor's representation to them of the obligations the government felt itself under to the college, owing to the peculiar circumstances under which the building had been destroyed,[2] and his assurance that such permission should in no event be advanced as a precedent for other lottery acts.[3] And when, seven years later, another act[4] was passed appointing new managers for this lottery, in place of some deceased and others unwilling to serve, Governor Hutchinson was careful to explain to their lordships that "the act which this act referred to was assented to by Governor Bernard upon special license from his Maj^ty^ and the execution of it has been delayed, the Lotteries for finishing a Town Hall in Boston interfering."[5]

[1] June 25th, 1765–'6, chap. 21, Acts and Resolves, IV., 834–'5.

[2] The dormitory caught fire from one of the fires kindled for the general court, which had adjourned to Cambridge on account of small-pox in Boston.

[3] To strengthen his request, Governor Bernard called the attention of the lords to the good results obtained by lotteries in Pennsylvania, the "Academy at Philadelphia" receiving a great part of its support from an annual lottery. See Acts and Resolves, IV., 868, note to 1765–'6, c. 21.

[4] July 2nd, 1772–'3, c. 16; Acts and Resolves, V., 212–'3.

[5] Governor Hutchinson to Lords of Trade, August 10th, 1772; Massachusetts Bay, B. T., Vol. 81, O. o., 48. For the scheme in detail of this lottery, see Acts and Resolves, V. 267, quoted from Executive Records of Council, 1765–'74, p. 650.

§ 82. *Events Leading to its Revival.*

For six eventful years the province of Massachusetts Bay now managed its financial affairs without resort to the seductive expedient of a lottery. The Boston massacre in 1770, had greatly excited the people; the destruction of the tea in Boston harbor in 1773, the opposition to the port bill in 1774, the representation of the colony in the general congress, the seizure of the arsenal at Charlestown by the militia, the adjournment of the general court to Concord and its reorganization there as a provincial congress, were the most prominent events immediately preceding the revolution. The first blood of that war was shed upon Massachusetts soil; the battle of Bunker Hill followed, and the colony was fairly involved in the war more than a year before the declaration of independence. The attitude that Massachusetts assumed upon the question of declaring independence, and the part she took in the struggle to make independence a fact, are not matters of dispute. The expenses of the colonial government were now enormously increased, and every expedient had to be tried in order to meet them. The taxes had been greatly augmented. Loans had been contracted in increasing amounts. In 1775 the first of a new series of bills of credit had been issued. Three years after the first blood of her citizens had been shed in the cause of American freedom, Massachusetts again turned to the lottery as a means of raising funds for continuing the war.

§ 83. *Tentative Lottery Legislation.*

On April 28th, 1778, the house of representatives, in recommitting the report of a committee appointed the day before, to report a resolve for giving the soldiers of the Massachusetts contingent in the continental army thirty pounds each, directed the committee to bring in besides a resolve for granting the gratuity, another for raising by lottery the sum of two million dollars. On the 30th the committee reported two resolves, according to instructions, except that in the latter resolve the amount to be raised by lottery was fixed at one million nine hundred and ninety-eight thousand dollars, from the sale of three classes of tickets (numbering one hundred and eleven thousand each), at four, six and eight dollars each, respectively, according to a scheme laid down in the resolve. On May 1st, the resolves were recalled by the house and recommitted. A joint committee the same day reported two resolves, which were passed in concurrence; the one relating to the raising of the money by lottery being as follows:

"Whereas this Court have, this day, passed a Resolve for paying certain Gratuities to such Officers & private Soldiers who inlisted into the fifteen Continental Battalions raised by this State & who inlisted before the 15th day of August last, for the term of three Years or during the War, And as it is thought expedient that a Lottery or Lotteries should be set on foot for raising a Sum of Money for the purpose aforesd.

"Therefore Resolved, That a Sum, not exceeding Seven Hundred & fifty Thousand Dollars be raised by a Lottery or Lotterys, by a Deduction of fifteen ℔ Cent upon the Amount of the Ticketts.

"That Oliver Wendell Esqr. Mr Henry Hill, Thomas Crane Esqr. Caleb Davis Esqr. & Mr Ezekiel Lewis, or any three of them, shall be Managers of said Lottery or Lotteries, & who shall be Sworne to the faithful discharge of said trust, & shall give Bond to the Treasurer of this State, in the Sum of One thousand pounds each for the performance of the trust hereby reposed in them: which said Managers shall make, & publish in the Boston & Worcester News-Papers, & also in the Hartford Paper a Scheme for said Lottery or Lotteries, as soon as may be, agreeable to this Resolve; & they shall also therewith publish all necessary rules & regulations for the Management thereof; That all Prizes of Fifty Dollars & upwards, shall be paid by Treasury Notes for the amount of Such Prizes, bearing date the last day of drawing said Lottery (or each of 'em, if two), & payable, with Six ℔ Cent ℔ annum Interest, on the first day of Jany A D: 1783—; also, that all smaller Prizes shall be paid by said Managers in Money; & also that all Prizes shall be paid without any deduction."[1]

[1] Felt's Massachusetts Archives, Vol. 218, p. 419.

This resolve was supplemented by the act of June 16th, 1778,[1] "to prevent the Forging, Altering or Counterfeiting the State Lottery Tickets," by which it was provided that any person convicted of being a party to the circulation of counterfeit tickets "shall be punished by being set on the gallows for the space of one hour, with a rope round his neck, and shall pay a fine not exceeding one thousand pounds, at the discretion of the court before whom the conviction may be, to the use of this state; and suffer not more than twelve months' imprisonment, nor less than three; and be publicly whipped, not exceeding thirty-nine stripes; or shall suffer only a part of the aforesaid punishments, at the discretion of the court before whom the conviction shall be, according to the circumstances of the offence; and shall pay to the person or persons defrauded treble damages;" and a reward of thirty pounds was offered for information leading to conviction.

§ 84. *The Great Lottery of 1778.*

Of the seven hundred and fifty thousand dollars which was the limit of the sum to be raised under the foregoing resolve, the managers attempted to raise only one hundred and forty-three thousand dollars—that being the specified percentage on nine hundred and fifty thousand dollars, the total value of the tickets offered for sale. The Lottery was arranged in four classes.[2]

A resolve of September 26th, 1778, directed the managers to take the most effectual methods for disposing of the tickets

[1] 1778–'9, c. 5.

[2] The scheme of the first class of this lottery was advertised as follows:

"THE General Assembly having passed a Resolve for raising a Sum of Money, not exceeding 750,000 Dollars, for the Benefit of those Officers and Soldiers who inlisted into the Fifteen Continental Battalions raised by this State, appointed *Oliver Wendell*, Esq; Mr. *Henry Hill*, *Thomas Crane*, Esq; *Caleb Davis*, Esq; and Mr. *Ezekiel Lewis*, Directors of a Lottery for that Purpose, who are sworn to the faithful Discharge of the Trust reposed in them.

"The following Scheme is accordingly offered to the Public, which it is hoped in the first class until the first day of December next, at which time, should any tickets remain unsold, the managers

will meet with their Approbation and Encouragement.

MASSACHUSETTS—STATE LOTTERY.

CLASS, NO. I.

Consists of 25000 Tickets, at 6 Dollars each, 6374 of which are Prizes of the following Value, *viz.*

No.		Dollars		Dollars.
1	of	4000	is	4000
1	of	2000	is	2000
2	of	1000	are	2000
10	of	500	are	5000
50	of	200	are	10000
100	of	100	are	10000
200	of	75	are	15000
460	of	50	are	23000
5550	of	10	are	55500
1 Exclusive of the above Prizes, the first Number shall be drawn, will be entitled to				300
2 The last drawn No. will be entitled to				200
6376 Prizes				127000
18624 Blanks				23000
25000 Tickets, at 6 Dollars				150000

"The Directors flatter themselves they shall be able soon to compleat the First Class, when they consider the Money to be raised is to be applied to the benevolent Purpose of rewarding those Officers and Soldiers who have endured Want, Hardship and Toil, and hazarded every Danger for the Safety of their Country, and who, when Government, through a Series of unfortunate Events, was unable in some Instances to comply with its Promises for their Support and Comfort, nobly scorn'd to shrink from the Post of Danger, and, like their great Leader, resolved never to survive the Ruin and Desolation of their Country.

"Public and seasonable Notice wlll be given of the Time and Place of Drawing, and when finished, a List of the Prizes will be published in the Continental Journal, and the Money will be paid (without any Deduction) to the Possessors of Benefit Tickets, (within twenty Days after a Publication of a List of Prizes) in the following manner, *viz.*

"All Prizes of Fifty Dollars and upwards will be paid in Treasurer's Notes for the amount of such Prizes, bearing Date the last Day of Drawing said Lottery, and payable on the first Day of January, 1783, with Interest at Six per Cent per Annum. All Prizes of Ten Dollars will be paid in Current Money.

"Prizes not demanded within Twelve Months after they are drawn, will not be were to take the numbers of such tickets, seal and deliver them to the state treasurer, and proceed at once to the drawing.[1]

§ 85. *Successive Classes.*

By January 26th, 1779, the managers were ready to proceed to dispose of tickets of the second class, and a resolve of that date[2] directed them to proceed with the sale with all possible dispatch, "and in order to Expedite the sale they are Directed to Lodge a Proportionable number of Said Tickets in the hands of Some Suitable Person in the Severall Towns in this State, and that the Sale be Continued until The seventeenth day of March next, unless the tickets are sooner disposed of * * * and the said Managers are hereby Directed to Proceed to the Drawing said Second Class without Delay, and it is further Resolved that the Managers of the said Lottery, be and they hereby are permitted To Receive for the Tickets in the Second Class of Said Lottery the Two Emissions of the Continental Curency Dated May 20th, 1777, and April 11th, 1778."

The drawing of the second class, advertised in the *Independent Chronicle* of February 4th, 1779, to commence March 17th, consisted of twenty thousand tickets at ten dollars each, five thousand seven hundred and fifteen of the tickets being prizes varying from one prize of five thousand dollars to four thousand two hundred and eighty prizes of fifteen dollars each. "The Managers having found a very great but needless expence to government, attending the drawing of the blanks in the first class, without the least advantage to the

paid, but will be deemed as generously given for the Purpose aforesaid, and will be applied accordingly.

"Tickets are to be had of the respective Directors at their Houses and Stores, where constant Attendance is given."—*Independent Chronicle*, June 25th, 1778. Quoted in Acts and Resolves, V., 1364.

[1] Felt's Massachusetts Archives, Vol. 219, p. 314.

[2] Printed Resolves, January session, 1779, ch. lxxx.

adventurers," it was announced that only the prizes would be drawn in this class. On March 1st, the sale of the tickets of the second class being "nearly completed," the managers were empowered[1] to receive the above-described emissions of bills for tickets in the third class. The scheme of the third class, advertised in the *Independent Chronicle* of March 11th, consisted of twenty thousand tickets at fifteen dollars apiece, five thousand seven hundred and fifty-one of which were prizes, varying from one prize of ten thousand dollars to three thousand five hundred and fifty-six prizes of twenty-five dollars each. "The present Class being in many Respects better calculated for the Benefit of the Adventurers, than the two former Classes, the Managers doubt not of a ready Sale of the Tickets, * * *: They therefore propose to commence Drawing said Lottery by the Middle of May; and as many Persons were disappointed of purchasing in the Second Class, they have now an Opportunity of laying out their Money on better Terms, if they apply seasonably."

A resolve of May 3d, 1779,[2] directs the managers to proceed with the selling until the 20th inst., unless the tickets were sooner disposed of, and to proceed to the drawing without delay. The managers thereupon gave notice that the drawing would begin on the day aforesaid, in the representatives' chamber, and that after that date no tickets would be sold. Drawers of small prizes in the first and second classes were urged to purchase tickets in the third class speedily, or, if not inclined to purchase, they were requested to call for their prizes before June 1st, as it was "not probable the managers" would "be in cash, to discharge the same," between June 1st and August 1st, "they being obliged, at that time, to deposit the prescribed money (received for tickets) in the loan office." At this point occurred a temporary interruption in an undertaking which thus far had proceeded successfully and

[1] Felt's Massachusetts Archives, Vol. 221, p. 354.

[2] *Ibid.*, Vol. 222, p. 285.

continuously. The managers representing to the general court that they had commenced drawing the third class agreeable to the order of the general court, but that they were much embarrassed by the necessity of paying into the treasury the moneys received for the sale of tickets, which, "being of the dead Emissions," must be transferred into the loan office by June 1st, they were recommended to suspend the drawing of the third class till June 3d.[1]

The fourth class, advertised in the *Continental Journal and Weekly Advertiser* of July 1st, 1779, was a repetition of the third, which, the managers announce, "met with general approbation." The drawing was fixed by a resolve of October 5th, for the second Wednesday in December. The resolve was published by the managers, who, at the same time, earnestly requested their agents in the various towns of the state to exert themselves in the sale of tickets. Holders of benefit tickets in former classes were also urged to apply speedily for payment. But popular interest in the lotteries was beginning perceptibly to decline. On November 30th,

"It being Represented to this Court by the Managers of this States Lottery that by reason of the multiplicity of publick Busness in which they have Necessarily been Ingaged it will be out of their power to be ready to proceed to the Drawing the fourth Class of Said Lottery at the time which has been sett for that purpose and allso that a Considerable Number of Tickets still remains unsold—Therefore Resolved, that the Manegers aforesaid be & they hereby are directed to postpone the drawing the fourth Class of Said Lottery, until the 20th day of January Next * * * and it is Further Resolved that the managers aforesaid be & they hereby are directed to Suspend Carrying on any more Classes of Said Lottery."[2]

This postponement was immediately advertised by the managers, who again urged the drawers of prizes in the former classess to apply for the money, as it would not be

[1] Felt's Massachusetts Archives, Vol. 170, p. 130.

[2] Printed Resolves of the November session, 1779, Chapter cxix.

"in the power of the managers to pay off any prize in the first class, unless applied for before the 15th day of January next." In the *Independent Chronicle* of January 13th, 1780, the managers announced that they intended "Drawing the Fourth and last Class of said Lottery on the 26th of this Month, at the Selectmens Room in Faneuil-Hall." The last official record pertaining to this important and, on the whole, remarkably successful series of financial enterprises,[1] prior to the adoption of the state constitution and the inauguration of a new financial regime, is a resolve of March 24th, 1780,[2] directing the managers to pay into the public treasury a certain number of prizes drawn in the first class of the lottery which had not been demanded, and the time for paying which, according to the managers' publication, had expired, and to proceed in like manner with any prizes of the other three classes when the time for the payment thereof should have expired, "such prizes being deemed as Generously given to the State."

§86. *Late Minor Lotteries.*

Three other lotteries of less magnitude than the "state" lottery, grew out of the war before the inauguration of the government under the constitution. On May 1st, 1779, two petitions to the general court, representing, the one[3] that the destruction of buildings in Charlestown by the enemy fur-

[1] Printed Resolves, Chapter lxvii.

[2] The acts of February 11th, 1779 (1778–'9, c. 35), April 14th, 1779 (1778–'9, c. 42), and May 3d, 1780 (1779–'80, c. 45), empowered the state treasurer to issue his notes at 6% for sums not exceeding £21,450, £81,570, and £49,830 respectively, an aggregate of £152,850, or $794,250, with which to pay the prizes of $50 and upwards in these four lotteries. Had all the tickets in the four series been sold, the amount realized would have been $950,000, and 15% of this sum, the proportion allowed by the law for *all* the prizes, is only $142,500. But not quite all the tickets were sold, and among those sold only prizes of $50 and upwards were to be paid in treasurer's notes. The provision for $794,250 in treasurer's notes may therefore be considered unnecessarily ample.

[3] Original in Felt's Massachusetts Archives, Vol. 222, p. 249.

nished an opportunity to widen and straighten the streets of that town; and the other[1] that the war had ruined the business of the proprietors of the long wharf in Boston so that they were unable longer to maintain it in good repair, and each praying for the benefit of a lottery, were favorably acted upon in a resolve; and the lotteries were established by the act of June 23d,[2] "For Raising by Lottery the Sum of Sixty Thousand Pounds, for the Purpose of Widening and Amending the Streets of the Town of Charlestown; and also for Raising by Lottery the Sum of Two Hundred and Fifty Thousand Pounds, for the Purpose of Repairing the Long Wharfe in the Town of Boston." The schemes of these lotteries, which were quite similar to those of the other Massachusetts lotteries, were published in the *Independent Chronicle* of February 3d, 1780. By both the resolve authorizing the lotteries and the act appointing the managers, the commencement of the lotteries was forbidden till after the completion of the "state" lottery.

In the spring of 1780 the condition of the public road from Westfield "through that rough and but little cultivated Tract of Land, well known by the name of the Green Woods," to Great Barrington—the chief east and west artery of inland communication and transportation in the state—always bad, had become much worse from the increased use made of the road in transporting supplies of provisions and other public stores to the Continental army on the Hudson, as well as in transporting great quantities of commodities belonging to inhabitants of New York and western Massachusetts to the seaboard. The general court, therefore, acting upon a petition of certain inhabitants of Berkshire county and others, granted the petitioners leave, by a resolve of June 2d, to bring in a bill for establishing a lottery to raise money for repairing the road, although the state itself had already spent during the last two years over one thousand pounds sterling in the repair of the

[1] Original in Felt's Massachusetts Archives, Vol. 222, p. 251.

[2] 1779-'80, c. 4.

roads through the Green Woods. The bill introduced in accordance with this resolve for raising a sum of not more than one hundred thousand pounds sterling, was, after several commitments in both houses, passed as the act of June 14th,[1] "For Raising by Lottery the Sum of Two Hundred Thousand Dollars" for the purpose mentioned. To the growing disfavor with which lotteries were now held in the state, and which was plainly indicated by the increase in this act of the deduction to be made from the whole sum for prizes from the customary fifteen per cent. to twenty per cent., was added in the present instance so strong a conviction, on the part of many, that the money to be raised would be used for personal rather than public advantage, that at least one petition[2] praying for the repeal of the act was sent to the general court, and three of the five managers designated by the act declined to serve. "Nothing but the most urgent necessity to effect a purpose of public utility," argue the three managers, "can justify the raising money by Lottery." And again: "Lotteries are a Burden in the community." These protests were unavailing, and the vacancies were filled by the selection of new managers; but before the lottery could be completed the state constitution went into effect.

[1] 1780, c. 1.

[2] Original in Massachusetts Files, "House," No. 640.

CHAPTER IV.

CURRENCY AND BANKING.

§ 87. *Colonial Paper Money: Massachusetts.*

The paper money of the Anglo-American colonies has been less neglected by writers upon fiscal topics than most other features of their financial history. We shall not here enter into a detailed account of the Massachusetts bills of credit. We can only summarize their history and record our impressions of the financial policy in which they played so prominent a part.

The policy of the government's issuing paper obligations in Massachusetts antedates somewhat the provincial charter. It was to provide for the payment of her colonial troops, and to meet other charges incurred in the unsuccessful expedition against Canada, in the inter-colonial war between the possessions of France and England, in 1690, and amounting in all to the sum of forty thousand pounds sterling, that, for the first time in the history of any of the colonies, the government of Massachusetts issued treasury notes, payable in one year, with the plausible idea of merely anticipating for a few months the payment into the treasury of the annual tax.[1] Although punctuality in redeeming these notes was observed for a number of years, the pressure of public expenses arising from the

[1] For some characteristic arguments in support of the action of the government in issuing the bills of credit, and in favor of the substitution of "paper money" for "stampt silver," see copious extracts in Trumbull's "First Essays at Banking," from the rare pamphlet, "Some Considerations on the BILLS OF CREDIT now passing in New England" (Boston Athenæum Tracts, c. 55), the authorship of the two parts of which Trumbull attributes to the Rev. Cotton Mather and Capt. John Blackwood respectively.

Indian wars, which for the first quarter of a century of its history almost continuously distressed the province, induced the general court, in 1704, to extend the time of redemption by taxes to two years, afterwards to a longer period, and finally to thirteen years. It is impossible to say how much farther this process of discounting the future might have been carried, had not a check been placed upon the operations of the court by royal instructions limiting the period for redeeming tax-bills to the year 1741, and prohibiting the issue of new ones until all those outstanding should be redeemed, except by acts subject to the king's approval before they should take effect.

§ 88. *Postponement of Payment.*

The idea in arranging the postponements was so to distribute the taxes over a number of years that the burden to be borne by the taxpayers in any one year would be sensibly lessened. With this end in view, the taxes pledged for the redemption of bills, and falling due from year to year, were so arranged that for several years subsequent to 1715–6 the amount to be raised for this purpose was exactly twenty-two thousand pounds sterling per year. Then for several years the amount annually called for was only sixteen thousand or seventeen thousand pounds sterling; then, when the natural effects of such a cumulative system began to be felt, it rose to twenty-four thousand pounds sterling, and even much more; though the average per year for a period of over forty years, or until 1757–8, when the last of the bills were redeemed through the operation of other causes and a different financial policy, was something less than twenty-eight thousand pounds sterling. There were some exceedingly wide divergences from this average; for example, in 1739–40, and in 1741–42, for neither of which years were any taxes at all pledged; in 1725–6, when taxes to the amount of over seventy-eight thousand pounds sterling were mortgaged; and in 1748–9, for which unfortunate year taxes to the amount of no less than one hundred and three thousand, eight hundred and sixty-eight pounds, five shillings, were pledged. The royal instructions had before this been disregarded under the pressure of increased expenses, and they were finally withdrawn at the earnest solicitation of the governor.

§ 89. *Two Opposing Policies.*

As soon as the mortgaged taxes began to fall due, the same reluctance to resort to actual taxation that had led to the introduction of the treasury notes in the last decade of the seventeenth century again manifested itself in propositions to levy only a portion of the amount due in taxes, and to trust to other sources of public revenue—to the imposts, the excises, tonnage and lighthouse tolls—for the remainder. These propositions invariably came from the house of representatives, and were as invariably opposed by the governors and their councils. The reasons for an opposition which, while it was for many years unavailing, was based on sound financial and moral principles, are nowhere better stated than in a speech of Gov. Joseph Dudley, to the house of representatives, in answer to repeated attempts on their part to reduce the amount named in the tax-bill of 1715–6 from twenty-two thousand pounds sterling, the sum which had been pledged for that year, to one-half that figure.

"At the last session of this Assembly," said the governor, "I earnestly recommended to you the raising of twenty-two thousand pounds sterling, granted and determined by two former assemblies of the Province, for the drawing in of that sum of the Province bills raised and emitted for the support of the late war and troubles with the Indians, which said acts of Assembly[1] were passed by the Representatives and the Council, and presented to the Governor to be signed and passed the seal in due manner, and accordingly in that form are sent home and are there recorded and accepted by the

[1] October 25th, 1710; May 30th, 1711.

Right Honorable Lords of the Council of Trade and Plantations, as I was commanded by the instructions for the Government; of which everybody concerned being apprized, I made no doubt you would without delay have proceeded to apportion and levy it, as those acts direct, as also the Impost and Excise, which are thereby in like manner determined to be raised, in aid of the said taxes severally. You are also sensible how well and thriftily, as also successfully, those sums were disbursed and applied to defray the necessary expenses of the war, and with what honor your Bills passed for the support of such heavy charges, without any disparagement, and it is easy to see how the credit of those Bills must needs sink and fail, if the present or any future Assembly shall upon any pretense whatever, break in upon those clauses in the said Acts for the time of payment, which I am willing to give my opinion we have no power, to do, nor have we any reason to project it; for that we are in peace and very capable to discharge our debts, in such proportions as they are determined. And since we have neither power nor need to delay the payment, I am of opinion we shall discourage the public faith of the Province to that degree, that our Bills will fail in their value, to the very great injury of everybody that have taken them, or are in possession of them. And in this we are justified by his Majesty's most gracious speech from the Throne—'That nothing can contribute more to the support of the credit of the nation than a strict observance of Parliamentary engagements.' I therefore earnestly recommend the consideration of the Tax, Impost and Excise to your present Resolves, and hope you will make no delay, but pass through them in two or three days, not admitting any other business this session."

§90. *The Policy of the Representatives.*

The house remained unmoved, and the bill was passed for a tax of eleven thousand pounds sterling. Similar proceedings in succeeding years ended in the same way. The financial policy thus forced upon the government by the provincial house of representatives, and persisted in by that body for nearly half a century with great show of jealousy for the maintenance of its alleged perogative in controlling the financial affairs of the province, has never received from historians the attention it deserves. If simplicity were the only requisite of a commendable fiscal policy, that of the Massachusetts house of representatives would deserve nothing but commendation. It consisted simply in a persistent refusal to raise by direct taxation one penny more than a sum calculated, not always accurately, to be just sufficient, when added to all the other revenues of the province, to cancel maturing obligations, and in the abandonment of the constantly-increasing current expenses of the government to be met by larger and larger issues of bills of credit. A careful tabulation of the financial transactions of the province from 1715 to 1757 shows that only once during the whole period of forty-two years did the budget contain an appropriation for running expenses,[1] and once provision for including in the tax a sum unappropriated,[2] and that only once was there an unanticipated surplus (1756–'57, three thousand pounds sterling, three shillings and four pence).

§ 91. *Banking Schemes.*

With the extension of the period for the redemption of the treasury notes, depreciation set in—not on account of a redundancy of paper money, but owing to the impairment of public confidence in the solvency or in the good faith of the government. The lack of acquaintance, on the part of the provincial financiers, with the principle which had already been formulated in Gresham's law, did not prevent the rapid disappearance, in accordance with the workings of that principle, of gold and silver money from the province, when they were brought into competition with a medium of less exchange value, even in quantities comparatively small at first; nor did it prevent the consequent contraction of the currency to an embarrassing degree. The rise of exchange with England and all other countries, which by 1713 had become con-

[1] June, 1752–'3, £8,142 4s.

[2] 1753–'4, £4,250.

siderable, was attributed to the general bad state of trade, this in turn being ascribed to the scarcity of a circulating medium rather than to its true cause, the disturbing influence of a depreciated currency. It was therefore thought that the most obvious way of striking at the root of the trouble was to increase commercial activity by the issue of more paper bills.[1] The historian Hutchinson,[2] himself a participant in the discussions of the house of representatives and the leader of a small but important party who proposed the heroic measure of drawing in the paper money and depending upon barter until the exiled coin could be recalled in the natural course of export trade, tells us that there were two principal schemes before the country for increasing the paper currency. A very numerous party had revived a project, originally published in London, in 1684, for the issue, by an incorporated company, of bills of credit which all the members of the company should engage to receive, but at no ascertained value as compared with silver and gold, real estate to a sufficient value being bound as security that the company would fulfil its engagements. "This party," says Hutchinson, "generally consisted of persons in difficult or involved circnmstances in trade, or such as were possessed of real estate but had little

[1] On March 3, 1700, the council negatived the report of a committee of the general court, recommending that the government strike copper pence, and that "a Sutable Number of Meet persons, with their Associates, their Heirs &c for the space of [blank] years, be allowed, appoynted, and impowred to Erect & Set up a Bank of Credit, & to make & Emit Bills of Credit, at their owne proper cost & charge, from two Shilling Bills to three Pound Bills, in such proportion as they see meet, to any vallue and not to take more then three ℔ c. ℔ ann. for Intrest.

"That all other persons be Inhibited making any of the Like Bills of Credit, or Seting up Such Bank dureing s[d] Terme.

"That no person shal or may buie any of s[d] Bills under the vallue therein exprest, on penalty of forfiting the Vallue of the same, so exprest in s[d] Bill or Bills."—Felt's Massachusetts Archives, Vol. 101, p. 184.

[2] The principal authorities for this period are Hutchinson and the pamphleteers. Trumbull speaks of "nearly thirty pamphlets and tracts printed from 1714 to 1721 inclusive, for and against a private bank or a public bank, the emission of bills of credit, and paper currency in general."—First Essays at Banking, p. 28.

or no ready money at command; and it may well be supposed that the party were numerous."

§ 92. *An Ideal Solution.*

Another party were happy in the belief that they had discovered an ideal solution of the problem in a plan by which the government should become its own banker, loaning its bills to any of the inhabitants who would mortgage their estates as security for the gradual repayment of the bills with interest, in a term of years, the interest, payable annually, to be applied to the support of the government—"an easy way of paying public charges, which," as Hutchinson says, "no doubt they wondered that, in so many ages, the wisdom of other governments had never discovered." The first party falling in with this scheme as the lesser of two evils, a bill was finally passed, though not until after a long struggle, in which the controversy spread throughout the province, dividing towns, parishes and families, for issuing fifty thousand pounds sterling, to be put into the hands of trustees and loaned on good security, for five years only, to any of the inhabitants, at five per cent. interest, one-fifth of the principal to be paid annually.

§ 93. *The Policy Determined.*

Thus was inaugurated a monetary policy which, not to go into details, it is sufficient to say was destined, in spite of constantly accumulating evidence of its utter viciousness, to become the accepted resort of an infatuated people, in every spasm of commercial embarrassment, for the next quarter of a century. So confident were its promoters of its entire sufficiency to the demands of the occasion that it was a matter of no difficulty to raise one thousand pounds sterling with which to purchase the resignation of one governor in order that another more favorable to the scheme might be appointed in his stead. The advice of Governor Shute, in his first message to the house, in 1716, that immediate measures be taken to correct the prevailing unhappy state of trade, was understood to mean nothing else than a further emission of bills of credit. The sum now to be issued, for the encouragement of husbandry, fisheries and other branches of trade, was made one hundred thousand pounds sterling in place of the previous fifty thousand pounds sterling; the time for repayment was extended to ten years instead of five; and, lest some portion of the province should be cheated of its share in the blessing about to be dispensed, it was provided that the whole sum, placed in the hands of commissioners appointed for each county, should be apportioned in the same ratio that the taxes were. In fact the most popular argument, if not the soundest, advanced in favor of the emission of the bills, was that the people might have something in which to pay taxes. The condition of trade had become distressing in the extreme, owing to what the most ardent inflationists confessed themselves willing to admit was a too hearty adoption of their policy by the other New England governments, especially by Rhode Island, which issued one hundred thousand pounds sterling in bills to loan to its inhabitants for twenty years. It is unnecessary to say that neither the Massachusetts emissions above referred to, nor an additional one of sixty thousand pounds sterling in 1627, when the time for repayment was extended to thirteen years, produced anything more than a temporary and delusive improvement in the state of affairs. A confederation of Boston merchants to protect themselves from the influx of foreign paper resulted in nothing better than the issue by the company of one hundred and ten thousand pounds sterling in notes redeemable in ten years in silver at ten shillings per ounce; so that at the end of the operation the nominal sum of paper in circulation in the province was greater than ever before, and silver soon rose to twenty-seven shillings.

§94. *Effects of that Policy.*

Concerning the disastrous effects of the presence of such an immense mass of unstable public obligations upon trade and the general condition of the people, neither contemporary nor later writers have been silent. The printed and manuscript writings of the time—pamphlets, sermons, letters—are filled with graphic descriptions of the distress to which individuals and communities were reduced, and with vehement complaints against the wealthy and the influential in society and the state, who were believed to be, in some way not well understood, responsible for the general suffering.

"Trade," says the historian Minot, "was in a manner reduced to a state of barter, and above all, the temptation every man was under, almost in self defense, to avail himself of an advantage in his contract, not guarded against by the parties at the time when it was made, was daily corrupting the morals and good faith of the whole body of people. One class censured another for these results. As trade has the first control over and is first affected by currency, so the merchants seemed to stand foremost for censure. Had they adhered to the laws for supporting the credit of the bills, by giving no more for silver and gold than the several governments [of the New England colonies] had valued them at, and so putting no additional advance upon their goods, the husbandman and the tradesman, it was said, would not have been obliged to raise the prices of product and labor. The assembly shared in the reproach for issuing a currency in its nature unstable and incapable of remaining at par."

The disastrous effects of this depreciation were felt most severely by the class of those who had some money at interest, or who depended for their support upon fixed incomes. The Rev. Daniel Appleton, in his fast-day sermon, 1748, instances as a case typical of many in the land, that of "an ancient widow whose husband died more than forty years ago, who had three pounds sterling a year settled upon her instead of her dower, which three pounds sterling would at that day and at the place where she lived procure towards her support the following articles: two cords of wood, four bushels of Indian corn, one bushel of rye, one bushel of malt, fifty pounds of pork, sixty pounds of beef, which would go a considerable way towards the support of a single woman. Now she can at most demand but seventeen shillings and three pence new tenor, which is about one-eighth her original three pounds, and be sure won't purchase more than one half or one quarter of the above necessaries of life; and this she must take up with, because there is no remedy in law for her."[1]

§ 95. *A Project Revived.*

It was at this juncture (1739) that the remnant of that party whose zeal and resentment had only been increased by the apparent success of their opponents in 1714 and 1716, again came forward with their favorite scheme of a private company empowered to issue bills of credit secured by pledges of real estate. To Thomas Hutchinson belongs the credit of first presenting to the people of the province the policy which, as the successor of the miserable expedient of inflation so long persisted in, was destined at no distant day to vindicate itself as the true policy for a state involved in extraordinary financial embarrassment. Hutchinson, as he had done on the former occasions, again urged the withdrawal of all the bills in circulation, proposing to borrow in England, upon interest, and to import into the province a sum in silver sufficient to redeem them from their possessors and so to furnish the inhabitants with a stable medium sufficient in quantity to meet all the demands of trade, while the equal distribution of its repayment over a long period of years would render the burden of consequent taxation tolerable. But the proximity of the year 1741, which, as the limit beyond which the royal instructions had prohibited the postponement of the payment of the bills of credit, had been burdened with taxes amounting to nearly thirty thousand pounds sterling, or ninety thousand pounds in paper, counter-balanced any sentiment which the unhappy experience of the people during the

[1] Quoted by Minot, History, I., p. 85.

last twenty-five years may have created in favor of hard money, and the proposition was rejected with something approaching unanimity; since the absence of instructions against the emission of bills of credit by private companies, left the way open for the continuance of the practice of inflation under conditions which were believed to promise results less disastrous than those which had been entailed by unlimited government issues.

§ 96. *The Land Bank Party.*

Hutchinson says that the "notable company" of eight or nine hundred persons at the head of which the projector of the land bank proposed in 1714 now placed himself, and which was to give credit to one hundred and fifty thousand pounds sterling of lawful money to be issued in bills, while it included some few of rank and good estate, was mainly composed of plebeians, persons of low condition and small estate, many of them, perhaps, insolvent. Each member was to pledge real estate in proportion to the sums he subscribed for and took out, or, if he possessed no real estate, to give a bond with two sureties, no personal security of more than one hundred pounds to be taken from one person. Every subscriber was to pay three per cent. interest on the sum withdrawn, and one-fifth of the principal yearly. There were to be ten directors and a treasurer, chosen annually. Payments of principal and interest might be made in bills, or in products and manufactures of the province, "or *Logwood*, though from *New Spain*," at such rates as the directors might set from time to time—a feature no doubt suggested by the colonial practice of receiving taxes in "country pay," and which gave to the new project the popular name of the "manufactory scheme." Such was the project urged before the general court in 1740, on the plea that, by the furnishing in this way of a medium and instrument of trade, not only would the inhabitants in general be better able to procure province bills for the payment of taxes;[1] but foreign and inland trade would be quickened and invigorated. Even in 1714 the number of those in favor of a private land bank had been so large that they were defeated only by the amalgamation of the hard money party with the public bank party; and it had ever since been steadily increasing. Beside the eight hundred subscribers to the bank now proposed, the needy portion of the province in general were favorable to the scheme. Indeed, it was soon clear that the great majority of the house of representatives were either subscribers or friends of the project, and it has ever since been known as the "land-bank house." The company was incorporated, and although, as Hutchinson tells us, "men of estates and the principal merchants of the province abhorred the project and refused to take the bills" of the company, an agreement among the merchants to issue for circulation their own notes redeemable in silver or gold at distant periods,[2] much like the scheme of 1733, was attended with no better results than that had been; for "great numbers of shopkeepers, who had long lived on the fraud of a depreciating currency, and many small traders gave the bills credit."

§ 97. *Land Bank Troubles.*

The dangers inherent in such a concern now began to be manifest. "The directors—it was said by vote of the company—became traders, and issued what bills they thought proper, without any funds or security for their repayment. They purchased every sort of commodity, however much of a drug it might be, for the sake of putting off bills; and by one means or another a large sum, perhaps fifty thousand pounds sterling or sixty thousand pounds sterling, was soon in circulation."[3] What was to be done? The well-meant

[1] Minot, History, I., says, "for the ostensible purpose of supplying a currency when the bills of credit issued by the government should be absorbed."

[2] Minot, I., says, "payable on demand in silver, or bills of credit equivalent, according to the current rate."

[3] Hutchinson, History of Masachsusetts II.

efforts of Governor Belcher to blast the bank[1] probably approached too near to an illegitimate exercise of authority to make very much head against a project with which perhaps a majority of the inhabitants of the province were in open or secret sympathy. A last resort remained in an appeal to parliament, whose power to control all public and private persons and proceedings in the colonies, our loyalist historian[2] cannot refrain from reminding us, no one then ventured to dispute. Here sounder financial views obtained; and the efforts of an agent to convince the committee that the course of the directors was justifiable, failed completely.

§ 98. *The Land Bank Doomed.*

The declaration of parliament that the act of 6 George I., Chapter 18, prohibiting the emission of bills of credit by private corporations in England, did, does and shall extend to her colonies and plantations in America, fell like a thunderbolt upon the bank. Nor was this all. Not only was the bank dissolved by the act, but the holders of its bills were given the right of action against every director or partner for the recovery of the sums expressed on their face, together with interest. In the despair of the moment, some of the partners were for defying the law and continuing the issue of bills; but calmer counsels prevailed, and the directors, realizing the paralyzed condition of the company, for once adopted the wisest course in throwing themselves upon the mercy of the general court. The business of winding up the disordered affairs of this unfortunate institution hung like a millstone about the neck of the court for many years, it being impossi-

[1] "Not only such civil and military officers as were directors or partners, but all who received or paid the bills, were dismissed. The governor negatived the person chosen speaker of the house because he was a director of the bank, and afterward negatived thirteen newly elected councilors who were directors or partners, or reputed to favor the scheme."—Hutchinson, II. See also Belcher's speech, November 22nd, 1740, and January 9th, 1741.

[2] Hutchinson, II.

ble, from the nature of the case, even in the end to do more than mete out conventional justice in a rough and unsatisfactory way to the legal representatives of those individuals who had been defrauded by the insidious dishonesty of the directors. We are not concerned now with the question of the constitutionality of these clauses in the above mentioned act, which gave to an enactment of twenty years before a meaning and intent from the date of its passage differing from those presumed to have existed in the minds of its originators, and which, by making these partners of the company severally liable for the redemption of all the bills issued since the incorporation of the company, created between the partners and the holders of the company's bills a relationship differing from that claimed to have been established by the instrument of incorporation. What is sufficiently plain is that the sound financier must strongly commend the action of parliament in refusing to be influenced by those arguments always advanced by the makers of bills that depreciate—especially by that time-worn and specious argument of the injustice of protecting mere speculators at the expense of those who have felt obliged to part with the bills at a discount—to make the amount of liability less than the face of the bills. If our state and national financiers, when called upon to deal with similar problems half a century later, had followed the example here set, they would have enjoyed a higher reputation to-day for honesty and sagacity. As between the two methods of inflation which had now been successively tried in Massachusetts, our choice must be decidedly for the former; for if that scheme was objectionable in that it hampered the government with some of the most perplexing questions of banking, the latter was still more so in that it endowed a banking company with some of the most important functions of government.

§ 99. *Inherent Evils.*

Not the least of the evils inherent in an irredeemable currency is the inequality in the distribution among the holders of it of losses and gains consequent upon the impossibility of graduating the quantity of it in circulation to the commercial needs of the community. Successive expansions and contractions of the circulating medium are ordinarily due to causes only in a limited degree, and after the lapse of a considerable time, susceptible to modification by political influences. Even when they are brought about by direct act of the government, they are dictated by motives other than, if not inconsistent with, that of preserving the financial equilibrium already existing among the people. It is, therefore, impracticable for the government, in the one case to prevent, or in the other to avoid producing, those changes in the numerical relation between the volume of paper in circulation and the volume of business to be done, by every one of which a fortuitous and demoralizing change in the relative values of all men's property is wrought. Had not the people of Massachusetts during a period of more than thirty years been schooling themselves to endure with whatever of equanimity they might be able the ill effects of such a system, the foundations of social order among them would have been seriously shaken if not overturned by the violent transition from the contraction that followed the collapse of the land bank to the expansion made necessary by the wars of Shirley's administration. The very cause of their embarrassment, however, was to become the means of their relief.

§ 100. *The Redemption of the Bills.*

The efforts made by the New England colonies, especially by Massachusetts, in the late expedition against Cape Breton, were so extraordinary that an equitable claim arose upon Parliament for compensation.[1] The province agent was successful in his effort to convince that body, through the committee to whom the petition of Massachusetts for reimburse-

[1] Minot, History.

ment was referred, that the depreciation in value which the bills had undergone was as much a charge upon the people as though it had been levied in the form of a tax; and the question of the amount for which the province should be reimbursed was happily settled in favor of a sum in sterling equal to the face value of the bills issued to meet the expenses of the expedition against Cape Breton. A threatened division among the ranks of the hard-money men at home was produced by the introduction in the house of representatives of a bill suggested by Hutchinson, now speaker of that body, by which it was proposed to make a speedy end of the bills of credit by applying the one hundred and eighty thousand pounds sterling of coin expected from England to redeeming, at the rate of eleven for one—the lowest rate of exchange in London for one or two years previous—one hundred and ninety-eight thousand pounds sterling of the two million two hundred thousand pounds sterling then outstanding, and laying a tax upon the year 1749 to sink the remaining two hundred and twenty thousand pounds sterling. The disruption of the party was happily averted by compromise; while, from the fact that the Hutchinson bill, as finally submitted and passed, was conditioned on the grant by parliament of the one hundred and eighty thousand pounds sterling, a contingency at a distance and not altogether certain, but little opposition was encountered from those who feared a derangement of trade from the substitution of coin for paper. The news which was received soon afterward, that the grant had actually been made by parliament, was greeted with more threatening demonstrations; but the arrival of the money produced no embarrassment except in those colonies, such as Rhode Island and Connecticut, whose governments declined the invitation of Massachusetts to conform their currency to hers. Successive grants by parliament for other expenses incurred by the province in defense of the king's government, supplemented by more liberal taxes on the part of the people, enabled the government to sink the last of its bills of credit in 1757–58, and the spectre of inflation was laid for more than a quarter of a century.

§ 101. *The Transition to Loans.*

Hutchinson briefly sketches the history of the transition from the bills-of-credit policy in Massachusetts to the loan policy. From the first introduction of paper money, says that ardent advocate of coin, it had been the custom of the government to provide for public charges by an issue of bills, and to grant a tax for the payment of the sum issued, to be levied and collected into the treasury in future years. The bills being all exchanged now for silver imported from England, and provision being made by law that no bills of credit should ever afterwards pass as money, there was difficulty in providing money for the immediate service of the government, until it could be raised by tax. Few people were at first inclined to lend to the province, although they were assured that they would be paid in a short time with interest. The treasurer was therefore ordered to make payment to the creditors of the government in promissory notes, payable to bearer in silver in two or three years, with lawful interest. This was really better, continues our historian, than any private security; but the people who had seen so much of the bad effects of the former paper money from depreciation, could not consider this as without danger; and the notes sold for silver at a discount, which continued till it was found that the government punctually performed its promises. From that time public security was preferred to private, and the treasurer's notes were more sought after than those of any person whomsoever. This was the era of public credit in Massachusetts Bay.[1]

§ 102. *The Loan Policy Established.*

In accordance with the policy thus inaugurated, a loan of

[1] Hutchinson, History of Massachusetts III., p. 10.

five thousand pounds sterling was authorized by the act of June 21st, 1750;[1] and during the thirty years immediately following no fewer than fifty other loans were authorized, in sums varying as widely as from two thousand one hundred and fourteen pounds sterling in 1754–5[2] to one hundred and ninety-seven thousand pounds sterling in 1765–6,[3] the only departure from the loan policy during this period being an issue of ten thousand pounds sterling in bills of credit in 1753–4.[4] In 1761 two issues of bills were made, one on January 31st,[5] of thirty thousand pounds sterling, and the other on April 18th,[6] of forty thousand five hundred pounds sterling; and shortly after,[7] a third issue of sixty thousand pounds sterling was authorized—all three on the strength of parliamentary grants not yet received. The political events of 1775, completely changing the financial relation of the provincial government to the English parliament, led not, indeed, to the abandonment of the loan policy, but to a revival along with it of a dependence upon bills of credit. A series of ten issues in 1775–6 and 1776–7, the smallest of which, twenty thousand pounds sterling,[8] and the largest, two hundred and six thousand pounds sterling,[9] were both passed on the same day, December 26th, 1776, again flooded the country with bills of credit to an amount of very nearly one million pounds sterling. Besides this, four loans aggregating two hundred thousand pounds sterling were authorized; and taxes aggregating nearly four hundred and seventy-five thousand pounds sterling were

[1] 1750–'1, c. 1.

[2] 1754–'5, c. 9.

[3] 1765–'6, c. 9.

[4] 1753–'4, c. 24.

[5] 1760–'1, c. 23.

[6] 1760–'1, c. 27.

[7] 1761–'2, c. 3.

[8] 1776–'7, c. 26.

[9] 1776–'7, c. 27.

laid—in all a sum of over one million five hundred thousand pounds sterling in two years—a portion of it, however, already depreciated. An earnest discussion, in 1777, of the proposal to call in all the bills of credit and substitute therefore interest-bearing treasury notes, ended in the issue of seventy-five thousand pounds sterling in such notes.[1] From 1778, in which year was passed the last act prior to the adoption of the federal constitution by Massachusetts for the emission of bills of credit, except in exchange, the policy of the commonwealth to raise money solely by loans and the revenue, which is mainly from direct taxes, was firmly established. Coeval with this event the history of Massachusetts as a British dependency ends, and the history of Massachusetts as a member of the American union begins.

[1] 1777–'8, c. 19.

CONCLUSION.

§ 103. *The Provincial Finances.*

That the mass of the people—those of the poorer sort comprising the majority—had gained little or no practical wisdom from the financial history of the colonial period, is evident enough from the history of the financial legislation of the provincial period; for now that the influence of the governor and council, owing to the change in their political relation to the house of representatives and to the people, wrought by the provisions of the provincial charter, was no longer paramount in legislation, it is to the influence of the representatives themselves that the prevailing character of that legislation is to be attributed. To the causes that combined to deplete the revenue under the colonial system—the timidity displayed in the financial legislation, the laxity of the financial administration and the practice of permitting taxes to be paid in "specie"—must now be added the long series of disagreements between these bodies, which, beginning almost as soon as the government was organized under the new charter, and continuing, with increasing bitterness, from time to time quite up to the revolutionary period, was the cause of very great embarrassment to the government and of prolonged suffering among the people.[1]

[1] It was fairly precipitated by the attempt of the house to cripple the power of the council by inserting in the bill for a tax upon polls and estates in July, 1703, a clause restricting draughts upon the treasury for incidental charges to £30. The controversy usually took the form of a refusal by the house to pass the tax acts, even when the taxes had been mortgaged by previous issues of bills of credit, unless the council would yield the point in dispute, whatever it might be. Between June, 1706, and September, 1731, the treasury was often empty for periods varying from a few weeks to two years at a time, owing to the refusal of the representatives to pass tax laws.

§ 104. *Criticism of the Policy.*

An unprejudiced review of this controversy throughout the period of its extent, the whole tedious history of which may be found scattered through the journals of the council and the house, leads to the conviction that the action of the council was uniformly more honorable, more sound financially, and better adapted to secure the prosperity of the province than that of the representatives, who, apart from a natural impatience at meeting with steady opposition to every one of those features of their usual policy of which mention has been made as doing much to deplete the colonial revenues, appear in nearly every instance of disagreement to have been actuated more by jealousy of the governor and council as representing the royal authority, than by any real appreciation of the financial needs of the hour, or, it must be confessed, by any genuine regard for the best interests of the commonwealth. Only on the hypothesis that a higher social ideal is realized when individualism is carried to such an extreme that debtors, on the sole ground of the excess of their numbers, may repudiate with impunity contracts voluntarily entered into with their creditors, and that one generation may recklessly discount the resources of the next, can the general financial policy of the house of representatives of the province of Massachutetts Bay be defended.

BIBLIOGRAPHY.

For the convenience of students, libraries where some of the rarer documents may be found are indicated.

A.—ORIGINAL DOCUMENTS.

1.—"A Brief Account of the Rise, Progress, and Present State of the Paper Currency of New England," etc. Boston: 1749.—American Antiquarian Society.

2.—"A Brief Account of the State of the Province of Massachusetts Bay. By a Lover of his Country." Boston: 1717. 12mo., pp. 8.

3.—"A Copy of the Kings Majesties Charter for Incorporating the Company of the Massachusetts Bay in New England in America. Granted . . . 1628." Boston: 1689. 4to., pp. 26.—Massachusetts Historical Society.

4.—"Act in addition to an Act entitled 'An Act to prevent Monopoly and Oppression.'" n. p., 1777. 8vo., pp. 8.

5.—"Act providing for the more easy Payment of the Specie Taxes," etc. n. p., 1786. 8vo., pp. 23.

6.—"Acts and Resolves of the Province of Massachusetts Bay." Published by the State. Boston: 1869, 1874, 1878, 1881, 1886. 8vo.

For that period in the history of the commonwealth during which the greatest, if not the most rapid, progress was made toward a realization in legislation of the normal forms of her financial activity in its leading departments, the "Acts and Resolves" furnish the best possible source of information. The value to the historian of Massachusetts finances, of the edition of these laws published by the state, is greatly enhanced by the copious and erudite notes by the editor, Mr. Abner C. Goodell.

7.—"Act to Restrain the Trade and Commerce of Massachusetts and other Provinces in America." n. p., 1774. Folio.

8.—"A Discourse concerning the currencies of the British Plantations in America, Especially with regard to their Paper money, more particularly in relation to the Province of the Massachusetts Bay in New England." Boston: 1740. 8vo., pp. 3+46.—American Antiquarian Society. Trumbull attributes this pamphlet to Dr. William Douglass.

9.—"A Letter from a Country Gentleman at Boston to his Friends in the Country." Boston: 1740.—American Antiquarian Society.

10.—"A Letter from a Gentleman in Boston, To his Friend in Connecticut." Boston: 1743. 4to., pp. 15.

A reply to "Heads proposed for an Act of Parliament, to regulate and finally suppress Paper Currencies in the N. E. Colonies," in which Rhode Island, for her enormous emissions of paper money, and the projectors of the land bank in Massachusetts, are severely censured.

11.—"A Letter from an Eminent Clergy-Man in the Massachusett's Bay, Containing some Just Remarks, and necessary Cautions, relating to Publick Affairs in that Province." Boston: 1720. 12mo., pp. (2) 13.

12.—"A Letter from One in the Country to his Friend in Boston, containing some Remarks upon a late Pamphlet, entituled, 'The Distressed State of the Town of Boston,'" etc. Boston: 1720. 12mo., pp. (2) 22.

13.—"A Letter Relating to a Medium of Trade in the Province of the Massachusetts Bay. Printed at the New Printing Office, opposite to the South East Corner of the Town House." Boston: 1740.—American Antiquarian Society.

14.—"A Letter to a Member of the Honorable House of Representatives on the Present State of the Bills of Credit." Boston: 1736. 8vo., pp. (2) 9.—American Antiquarian Society.

15.—"A Letter to —— Merchant in London, concerning a late Combination in the Province of Mass.-Bay, in N. E.,—to impose or force a Private Currency called Land Bank Money. Printed for the Publick Good." 1741.—American Antiquarian Society.

16.—"A Letter to the Merchant in London to whom is directed a Printed Letter relating to the Manufactory Undertaking, dated New England Boston Feb'y 21 1741 Printed for the Publick Good."

17.—"A Model for erecting a Bank of Credit," etc. London: 1688. 16mo., pp. (2) 30. Reprinted. Boston: 1714.

18.—"A Mournful Lamentation For the sad and deplorable Death of Mr. Old Tenor, A Native of New-England, who, after a long Confinement, by a deep and mortal Wound which he received about Twelve Months before, expired on the 31st day of March, 1750. . . . To the mournful Tune of Chevy Chace." By Joseph Green. Boston. n.d. Folio broadside.

19.—"An account of the Rise, Progress and Consequences of the Land Bank and Silver Schemes in the Province of Massachusetts Bay." Boston: 1744. 8vo., pp. 91.—Massachusetts Historical Society.

20.—"An Act for repealing Certain Parts of an Act postponing the Payment of Government Securities." Boston: 1781. 8vo., pp. 7.

21.—"An Act providing Remedy for Bankrupts and their Creditors, printed & referred to the People of the Province of Massachusetts Bay, April, 1757." n. p. 1757. 4to.

22.—"An Act to prevent Monopoly and Oppression." n. p. 1744. 8vo.

23.—"An Act to supply the Treasury with the Sum of Four Hundred Thousand Pounds Money." Boston: 1781. 8vo., pp. 8.

24.—"An Addition to the Present Melancholy Circumstances of the Province Considered. . . Exhibiting Considerations about Labour, Commerce, Money, Notes, or Bills of Credit." Boston: 1719. 16mo., pp. 28.—Library of Congress.

25.—"An Essay concerning Silver and Paper Currency more especially with regard to the British Colonies in New England." Boston: Between 1738 and 1740.—American Antiquarian Society.

26.—"An Inquiry into the Nature and Uses of Money; more especially of the Bills of Publick Credit, Old Tenor. With a Proposal of some proper Relief in the present Exigence. [And] A Reply to the Essay on Silver and Paper Currences [sic]." Boston: 1740. 8vo., pp. (2) 78.—American Antiquarian Society.

27.—"Another Letter, From One in the Country, to his Friend in Boston." Boston: 1714 [?] 4to., pp. 11.

28.—"Answer to an Advertisement in the Boston Gazette, Feb. 20, 1721, dated, N. E. Castle-William, February, 1720, 21." Boston: 1721.—Massachusetts Historical Society. Relative to paper money.

29.—"Appendix to Massachusetts in Agony. By Cornelius Agrippa, L. L." Boston: 1751. 4to., pp. 20.—Massachusetts Historical Society.

30.—"A Project for the Emission of an Hundred Thousand Pounds of Province Bills, in such a manner as to keep their credit up Equal to Silver, and to bring an Hundred Thousand Pounds of Silver Money into the Country in a few years." Boston: 1720.—American Antiquarian Society.

31.—"A Projection, for regulating the value of Gold and Silver coins, published in the Boston Evening Post, Dec. 14th, 1761; reprinted, to be prefixed to 'Considerations on Lowering the Value of Gold Coins, within the Province of Massachusetts-Bay.'" By Thomas Hutchinson. Boston: 1762. 8vo., pp. 8.

32.—"A Vindication of the Bank of Credit." Boston: 1714.

Subscribed by Samuel Lynde, E[dward] Lyde, John Colman, Elisha Cooke, jr., J[ohn] Oulton, Timothy Thornton, Oliver Noyes, William Pain, and Nathaniel Oliver—"certainly a fair representation of the business men of Boston at that time."—*Trumbull.* In answer to Dudley's "Objections."

33.—"A Vindication of the Remarks of One in the Country upon the distressed State of Boston, from some Exceptions made against 'Em in a Letter to Mr Colman." 1720.—American Antiquarian Society.

34.—"A Word in Season to all True Lovers of their Liberty and their Country; both of which are now in the utmost Danger of being forever lost. By Mylo Freeman," etc. Boston: 1748. 16mo., pp. 16 (4).

In opposition to Hutchinson's plan of appropriating the reimbursement money for the Cape Breton expedition, to redeem old tenor bills. See Hutchinson, History, ii, 392–'5.

35.—"A Word of Comfort to a Melancholy Country, or the Bank of Credit Erected in the Massachusetts Bay, Fairly Defended by a Discovery of the Great Benefit, accruing by it to the whole Province; With a Remedy for Recovering a Civil State when Sinking under Desperation by a Defeat on their *Bank of Credit.* By AMICUS PATRIÆ. . . . Boston: . . . 1721." 12mo., 1 leaf, 58 pp. American Antiquarian Society.

Attributed by general consent to the Rev. John Wise. "His arguments in favor of fiat paper-money—whether in the shape of bills of credit or bills of a private bank—may not seem of great force: but they were urged with such fulness of conviction, and with so much of the 'racy and dainty humor' that characterized the author of 'The Churches' Quarrel Espoused,' that they will amply repay perusal."—*Trumbull.* Copious extracts in Trumbull's "First Essays."

36.—"Chronicles of the Pilgrim Fathers of the Colony of Plymouth from 1620 to 1625." Edited by Alexander Young. Boston: 1844.

37.—"Chronicles of the First Planters of Massachusetts Bay from 1623 to 1636." Edited by Alexander Young. Boston: 1846.

These two books bring together accurate copies of many valuable documents previous to 1650, the originals of which are more or less inaccessible. They contain copious and learned notes.

38.—"Chronological Table of the most Remarkable Events in the Province of the Massachusetts Bay, from 1602 to 1770." Boston: 1771. 8vo., pp. 8.

39.—"Consideration on Lowering the Value of Gold coins within the Province of the Massachusetts Bay." Boston: 1761.—American Antiquarian Society.

40.—"Considerations on the Bank of North America." Philadelphia: 1785.—American Antiquarian Society.

41.—"Continuation of the History of the Province of Massachusetts Bay, from 1748." By G. Richards Minot. Boston: 1798, 1803. 2 Vols., 8vo.

42.—"Council Records." 97 MS. vols. in office of Secretary of State, Boston.

43.—"English Advice to the Freeholders . . of the Province of the Massachusetts Bay." Boston: 1722. 8vo., pp. (2) 6.

44.—"Enquiry into the State of Bills of Credit of the Province of the Massachusetts-Bay in New England; in a letter from a Gentleman in Boston to a Merchant in London." London: 1743. 8vo., pp. 52.—Library of John Carter Brown, Esq., Providence, R. I.

45.—"Exact Table, Shewing how Provisions ought to be sold when the Dollars pass for Six Shillings a piece, which they must do according to the Act of the General Court." Boston: 1750. 8vo.

46.—"Exact Table to bring Old Tenor into Lawful Money, from 15d to a Thousand Pounds," etc. Boston: 1750. 8vo.

47.—"General Court Records." 73 MS. vols. in office of Secretary of State, Boston.

Of these, Vols. I. to V. inclusive, have been printed in Shurtleff's edition of the "Massachusetts Records."

48.—"Geographical and Statistical View of Massachusetts Proper. By Rodolphus Dickinson. Greenfield: 1813."

"The author aspires at least to the merit of impartiality."—*Author's Preface.*

49.—"History of Massachusetts from the First Settlement Thereof in 1628–1774." By Thomas Hutchinson. Boston: 1795, 1828. 3 vols., 8vo.

Especially valuable for the last half of the eighteenth century. Though Hutchinson's patriotism has been violently impugned, his soundness upon financial questions cannot be gainsaid. In the troubled financial and political times in which his active life was passed, however he may have erred in his persistent allegiance to the British Crown, his voice was always powerfully raised in favor of a sound currency and conservative banking.

50.—"History of New England, from 1630 to 1649." By John Winthrop. Boston: 1853. 2 vols., 8vo.

The first Winthrop was a poor financier. His narrative is valuable in a financial connection more for the indirect light which it throws upon the closely related subjects of the social and economic condition of his colony and of New England in the earliest period of their history than for any specifically financial materials that it contains.

51.—"Journals of the House." Over 100 vols. of MS. and printed sheets in the office of the Secretary of State, Boston, and in the State Library.

52.—"Letter addressed to the Legislators of the Several States, composing the Federal Union recommending an uniform Continental Currency," etc. New York: 1796.—American Antiquarian Society.

53.—"Letter from one in Boston to his Friend in the Country, in answer to a Letter to John Burrill Esq. Speaker to the House of Representatives, for the Province of Massachusetts Bay in New England." Boston: 1714.—Boston Athenæum Tract C 121.

54.—"Massachusetts Archives." 244 MS. volumes in office of Secretary of State, Boston.

"The most extensive work which has ever been done on the Archives of the State was accomplished between 1836 and 1846 by the Rev. Joseph B. Felt . . . The result was 241 volumes [now 244] of what are known as the MASSACHUSETTS ARCHIVES . . . Having been subjected in parts to considerable wear in the forty years that had intervened, about one-half of them . . . were in 1882-3 repaired in binding . . . and they now rest in excellent order in the new cases in the Archive room."—*Report of Committee on Records*, 1885. An acquaintance with such of the vast number of original documents in these archives as bear upon his line of work is absolutely indispensable to any one essaying to write in any department of the history of Massachusetts. Together with the various other series of records in the custodies of the Secretary and the Treasurer of the Commonwealth, they form such a body of records, many of them now printed through the wise liberality of the state, and nearly all of them classified and indexed, as is possessed by no other American commonwealth.

55.—"Massachusetts, or the First Planters of New England, the end and manner of their coming thither, & abode there: in several Epistles. Boston, New England: 1696."

A rare pamphlet, sometimes known as "Dudley's Letter to the Countess of Lincoln," concerning "all our matters" in Massachusetts from the first settlement to the date of the writing, March, 1630–'1. The imperfect copy in the Columbia College library is without a title-page, and contains but 32 of the original 56 pages.

56.—"Money the Sinews of Trade. The State of the Province of the Massachusetts-Bay Considered with respect to its Trade for want of a Medium of Exchange sufficient to manage it," etc. Boston: 1731. 8vo, pp. 16.—*Fac simile* reprint in Lenox Library.

57.—"New News from Robinson Cruso's Island, in a Letter to a Gentleman at Portsmouth." Boston: 1720. 16mo., pp. 8.

"By an advocate of a large emission of bills of credit, and against the majority in the Council and the supporters of Gov. Shute in his contest with the popular party."

58.—"News from the Moon. A Review of the State of the British Nation," etc. Boston: 1721[?]. 16mo., pp. 8.

59.—"Observations occasioned by reading a Pamphlet, intituled, A Discourse concerning the Currencies of the British Plantations in America." London: 1741. 8vo., pp. 23.

60.—"Observations on the Finances of Massachusetts." Boston: 1786. 8vo.—American Antiquarian Society.

61.—"Observations on the Nature and use of Paper Credit and the peculiar advantages to be derived from it, in North America," etc. Philadelphia: 1781.—American Antiquarian Society.

62.—"Observations on the Scheme for 60,000 l in Bills of a New Tenour." Boston: 1738.—American Antiquarian Society.

63.—"Objections to the Bank of Credit lately Projected at Boston, being a Letter upon that Occasion, to John Burrill, Esq.; Speaker of the House of Representatives." By Paul Dudley. Boston: 1714.

A "Postscript" was added after the author was informed that "the Bankers had new modeled their Projection, and Reformed it, as they reckon, in two Articles." American Antiquarian Society. The objections "to a *private* bank of credit—a 'partnership bank,' 'set up and carried on without a *charter* from the Crown,' and 'without the knowledge and leave of his Majesty's Government of this Province'—were clearly presented and forcibly urged."—*Trumbull.*

64.—"Path to Riches. An Inquiry into the Origin and Use of Money, and into the Principles of Stocks and Banks, To which are subjoined some Thoughts respecting a Bank for the Commonwealth." By James Sullivan. Boston: 1792.—American Antiquarian Society.

65.—" Postscript to a Discourse concerning the Currencies of the British Plantations in America." 1740.—American Antiquarian Society.

66.—" Records of the Colony of New Plymouth." 12 vols. Boston: 1855, '6, '7, '9, '61. 4to.

67.—" Records of the Governor and Company of the Massachusetts Bay in New England." Boston: 1853–'4. 5 vols. 4to.

The transcription and printing of these two series of records by the state, a task involving a prodigious amount of labor, has rendered easily accessible the original records of the vast body of miscellaneous business which, during the seventy-two years covered by the colonial governments of Plymouth and Massachusetts Bay, came before the general courts for legislation or adjudication, including records of many matters properly belonging to the financial history of the commonwealth, of which records are not known to exist elsewhere.

68.—" Reflections On the Present State of the Province of the Massachusetts-Bay in General, And Town of Boston in Particular; Relating to Bills of Credit And to Support of Trade by Them: As the same has been lately represented in several Pamphlets." Boston: 1720. Sm. 8vo., pp. 22.—Boston Public Library.

69.—" Report on Direct Taxes." By Oliver Wolcott.—American State Papers, Vol. 7 (Finance, Vol. 1), No. 100.

70.—" Severals relating to the Fund Printed for divers Reasons, as may Appear." Boston: 1682.

" This tract is so rare that it apparently has escaped the observation of every Massachusetts historian or antiquary since the time of Thomas Prince. Perhaps no perfect copy of it is extant."—*Trumbull.* The one examined by the author of " First Essays," in the Watkinson Library, Hartford, Conn., " contains, on a single sheet in pot quarto, the first eight pages of the tract, and is without a separate title-leaf or imprint."

71.—" Some Considerations on the Bills of Credit now passing in New-England. Addressed unto the Worshipful, John Philips Esq. Published for the Information of the Inhabitants." Boston: 1691. 12mo., pp. 23.

" These 'Considerations' end on p. 9; and pp. 11–23 are occupied with 'Some Additional Considerations, Addressed unto the Worshipful Elisha Hutchinson, Esq. By a Gentleman that had not seen the foregoing Letter.'" " A noteworthy, but hitherto nearly unnoticed, pamphlet . . in support of the action of the government in the issue of bills of credit, and to advocate the substitution of 'paper money' for 'stampt silver.' . . . In these [last] few pages the emission of bills of credit is defended, and the advantages of a resort to paper as a substitute for silver are set forth with considerable ability and address."—*Trumbull.* Referred to by Felt as Boston Athenæum Tract C 55. Trumbull attributes the authorship of " Some Considerations" to the Rev. Cotton Mather, and that of " Some Additional Considerations" to Capt. John Blackwell.

72.—"Some Considerations Upon the several sorts of Banks Proposed as a Medium of Trade: and Some Improvements that might be made in the Province, hinted at." Boston: 1716. 8vo., pp. 16.

"Excessively rare."—*Trumbull.* Opposed to both private and public bank projects, and advocates the issue of public bills to be loaned to the towns at 5% interest.

73.—"Some Observations on the Bill intitled, An Act for granting to His Majesty an Excise upon Wines, and Spirits—distilled, sold by Retail or consumed within this Province, and upon Limes, Lemons, and Oranges." Boston [?]: 1754. 16mo.

74.—"Some Observations relating to the Present Circumstances of the Province of Massachusetts-Bay; Humbly offered to the Consideration of the General Assembly." Boston: 1750. 4to., pp. 20.

75.—"Some Proposals to benefit the Province." Boston: 1720.—American Antiquarian Society.

76.—"Speeches of the Governors of Massachusetts, from 1765 to 1775; and the Answer of the House of Representatives, to the same, With the Resolutions and Addresses for this Period." Boston: 1818.

Very scarce. Known as the "Massachusetts State Papers."—Boston Public Library.

77.—"The Case of His Majesty's Province of the Massachusetts Bay in New England, with respect to the Expences they were at in taking and securing Cape Breton." London: 1744. Folio, pp. 4.

78.—"The Colonial Laws of Massachusetts, reprinted from the edition of 1660, with Supplements to 1672. Also the Body of Liberties of 1641." Reprinted in *fac simile* by the state. Boston: 1889.

79.—"The Colonial Laws of Massachusetts, Reprinted from the Edition of 1672, with the Supplements through 1686." Reprinted in *fac simile* by the state. Boston: 1887.

80.—"The Crisis." By the Rev. Samuel Cooper. Boston: 1754. 8vo. Opposed to the "Excise Bill."

81.—"The Distressed State of the Town of Boston," etc. By John Colman. Boston: 1720.

82.—"The Distressed State of the Town of Boston Once more Considered. And Methods for Redress humbly proposed. With Remarks on the pretended Country man's Answer to. . . . The Distressed State of Boston &c. With a Schaeme for a Bank laid down: And Methods for bringing in Silver Money, Proposed." By John Colman. Boston: 1720. 16mo., pp. (2) 22.

83.—"The Eclipse." Boston [?]: 1754. 8vo., pp. 8.

Opposed to the bill "which requires every Person to render a publick Account of his private Consumption of Liquors, upon Oath." "Why are we so strenuously exerting our selves against the Encroachments of the French? Why are we plunging our selves into Debt by Armaments and Expeditions, but for the sake of Liberty? And what should we gain by all, could we suppose . . . the forces employed to defend us against a foreign Yoke must be paid by taxes as *grievous and oppressive* as the subjects of an arbitrary Power groan under?"—Pp. 4+5. Lenox Library. Not in the Brinley catalogue.

84.—"The Melancholy State of the Province considered in a Letter From a Gentleman in Boston, to his Friend in the Country." Boston: 1736.—American Antiquarian Society.

85.—"The Monster of Monsters: A true and faithful Narrative of a great Surprize and Terror of His Majesty's Good Subjects: Humbly Dedicated to all the Virtuosi of New-England. By Thomas Thumb, Esq." Boston: 1754. 8vo., pp. 24.

A satirical account of the debate in the Council upon the "Excise Bill," after its passage by the House. Ordered by the legislature to be burned.

86.—"The Path to Riches." Boston: c. 1750.

87.—"The Present Melancholy Circumstances of the Province Considered," etc. Boston: 1718–'19. 16mo., pp. 16.

88.—"Trade and Commerce Inculcated, in a Discourse Showing the Necessity of a Well-governed Trade, in order to a Flourishing Common-Wealth, With some proposals for the bringing Gold and Silver into the Country for a Medium of Trade [and] for supporting the Credit of the Paper-Currency. By Amicus Reipublicæ." Boston: 1731. 8vo., pp. 58.

B.—SECONDARY AUTHORITIES.

89.—"An Historical Account of Massachusetts Currency. By Joseph B. Felt, Boston: 1839." 8vo., pp. 259.

Perhaps the earliest writer to attempt a systematic presentation of any department of the financial history of Massachusetts, Mr Felt enjoyed exceptional opportunities for obtaining trustworthy information upon this subject from his long and very valuable connection with the records in the office of the secretary of state. The large mass of facts bearing upon the history of the Massachusetts currency, which makes his book indispensable to every investigator of the subject, was mostly gleaned from this source. The arrangement is a simple chronological one. The author's few attempts at the discussion of financial principles, though, like his narrative, lacking in literary merit, are in the main sound.

90.—"A History of the Bills of Credit or Paper-Money issued, by New York, from 1709 to 1789." By J. H. Hickcox. Albany: 1866.—American Antiquarian Society.

91.—"An Historical Sketch of the Paper-Money issued by Pennsylvania." By H. Phillips, jr. Philadelphia: 1862.—American Antiquarian Society.

92.—"Commentaries on the Laws of England." By Sir William Blackstone. Philadelphia: 1878. 8vo., 2 vols.

93.—"Historical Account of Connecticut Currency, Continental-Money, and the Finances of the Revolution." By Henry Bronson. New Haven: 1865.

In Vol. I., papers of the New Haven Colony Historical Society.—American Antiquarian Society.

94.—"Historical Collections, being a General Collection of Interesting Facts, Traditions, Biographical Sketches, Anecdotes, &c., Relating to the History and Antiquities of Every Town in Massachusetts. . . . By John Warner Barber. Worcester: 1841." 8vo., pp. 632.

95.—"Historical Memoir of the Colony of New Plymouth," 1620–1675. By Francis Baylies. Boston: 1830. 2 vols.

96.—"Historical Sketches of American Paper Currency." By H. Phillips, jr. 2 vols. Roxbury: 1866.—American Antiquarian Society.

97.—"Historical Sketch of Continental Paper Money." By S. Breck. Philadelphia: n. d.—American Antiquarian Society.

98.—"Historical Sketch of the Finances of Pennsylvania." By T. K. Worthington.

Vol. II., No. 2, of the Publications of the American Economic Association. A rather fragmentary summary of an interesting and instructive development in financial history.

99.—"History of Massachusetts, from the Landing of the Pilgrims till the Present Time." By George Austin. Boston: 1876.

100.—"History of Massachusetts from 1620 to 1820." By John Stetson Barry. Boston: 1855–'7. 3 vols.

101.—"History of the New York Property Tax." By John C. Schwab.

Vol. V., No. 5, of the Publications of the American Economic Association. The best sketch of the financial history of an American commonwealth that has yet appeared.

102.—"History of the United States of America." By George Bancroft. New York: 1885.

103.—"Notes on Ante-Revolutionary Currency and Politics." By A. H. Ward. Boston: 1860.

In July number *New-England Historical and Geneological Register.*

104.—"Public Debts; An Essay in the Science of Finance." By Henry C. Adams. New York: 1887.

105.—"Records of the Company of the Massachusetts Bay in New England. From 1628 to 1641. As Contained in the First Volume of the Archives of the Commonwealth of Massachusetts." Cambridge: 1850. 8vo., pp. cxxxviii+107.

Comprises Vol. III. of the "Transactions" of the American Antiquarian Society. The "Records" have since been printed entire by the state, but the "Prefatory

Chapter" of 138 pages, by Mr. Samuel F. Haven, contains more information concerning the history of the company prior to the transfer of the charter than has been brought together by any other writer.

106.—"Remarks on the Early Paper Currency of Massachusetts." By Nathaniel Paine. Cambridge: 1866.

107.—"Report of the Commissioners on the Condition of the Records, etc., in the Secretary's Department." Boston: 1885. 8vo., pp. 42.

Valuable as describing particularly many of the sources for original information concerning the history, both general and financial, of the commonwealth.

108.—"Statistics and Economics." By R. Mayo-Smith.

Vol. III, Nos. 4 and 5, of the Publications of the American Economic Association.

109.—"Taxation in American States and Cities." By Richard T. Ely. New York: 1888.

Like most of Professor Ely's work, popular and not unscientific.

110.—"The First Essays at Banking and the First Paper Money in New England." By J. Hammond Trumbull. Worcester: 1884. 8vo., pp. 40.

Privately reprinted from the Report of the Council of the American Antiquarian Society October 21, 1884. Valuable for period from 1650 to 1721. Based upon Hutchinson and Felt, Massachusetts public records, and rare pamphlets in the Boston Athenæum, the Library of the American Antiquarian Society, Worcester and the Watkinson Library, Hartford.

111.—"The General Property Tax." By Edwin R. A. Seligman.

Vol. V., No. 1, of "Political Science Quarterly."

112.—"The History of Tariff Administration in the United States." By John Dean Goss.

Vol. 1, No. 2, of "Columbia College Studies in History, Economics and Public Law."

113.—"The Puritan Commonwealth." By Peter Oliver. Boston: 1856. 8vo.

NOTE.—In the above bibliography no reference is made to works in general finance, such as those of Cohn, Leroy-Beaulieu, Roscher, Schäffle, Wagner, etc.